CONSPIRACY THEORIES

CONSPIRACY THEORIES

This edition copyright © Summersdale Publishers Ltd, 2020

First published in 1998 as *The A–Z of Conspiracy Theories*

Published in 2004 as *Conspiracy Theories*, reprinted 2005; new edition published in 2010, revised in 2015, and expanded and updated in 2020

With additional text by Johnny Morgan, Elanor Clarke and Lucy York

An Hachette UK Company
www.hachette.co.uk

Summersdale Publishers Ltd
Part of Octopus Publishing Group Limited
Carmelite House
50 Victoria Embankment
LONDON
EC4Y 0DZ
UK

www.summersdale.com

Printed and bound by CPI Group (UK) Ltd, Croydon, CR0 4YY

ISBN: 978-1-78783-565-8

Substantial discounts on bulk quantities of Summersdale books are available to corporations, professional associations and other organizations. For details contact general enquiries: telephone: +44 (0) 1243 771107 or email: enquiries@summersdale.com.

CONSPIRACY THEORIES

A Compendium of History's Greatest Mysteries and More Recent Cover-Ups

JAMIE KING

summersdale

IMPORTANT NOTE

The conspiracy theories contained in this book are just that: theories. The editor and the publishers make no claim that any of these theories have any basis in fact. They are merely theories that have at some point been expressed in the public domain. Such theories are reproduced herein for entertainment purposes only and are not intended to be taken literally.

CONTENTS

INTRODUCTION

The archetypal conspiracy theory might go something like this: there is a clandestine secret society in our midst... they are alien to all we believe in and are about to seize control of the world... they are everywhere... they are ruthless and powerful... they are sexually depraved... they perform the most heinous crimes known to humankind.

Belief in conspiracy theories is more than just the belief in an occasional underhand plot. It is a belief system that asserts that world events are being governed in secret by a group of ultra-powerful puppeteers behind the scenes. While little may be done about this apparent corruption, at least we can enjoy the satisfaction of having worked out what is going on.

Of course, one can argue that obsession with conspiracy theories serves only to demonstrate the lunatic paranoia running rife in today's society. Much talk about conspiracies is dismissed as paranoia and much of it *is* paranoia. But in reality, history has proved all too well that politicians lie, presidents lie and bureaucrats lie. If we continue to be gullible and believe everything that is presented to us, the truth will never come out. It becomes not only interesting and revealing but an absolute priority to question authority and, more specifically, the authoritarians.

Why is it that we can accept that Barack Obama is who he says he is? Or that the CIA assassinated the president of Chile, but we cannot believe that they would assassinate their own? Why is it we can accept that governments would experiment on their citizens with plutonium, syphilis and nerve gas, but don't consider that they would use the AIDS virus? Why did the German populace accept that Hitler was trustworthy in the first place?

Conspiracy theories are not new. It is believed that Emperor Nero concocted an elaborate tale to shift the blame to the Christians for the burning of Rome. Hitler was a master of such deceit. And, undoubtedly, when conspiracies fail to accurately predict world events, this only serves to prove their credibility. Double bluff is refined to an art form.

It cannot be denied that controversy has often accompanied the pivotal points of Western civilization. Many major events, for better or for worse, have occurred as the direct result of unseen people who have held the keys to the actions of the world. Startling discoveries, often stretching far back into history, can affect the very way our Western thought processes and behaviour patterns are conducted. And that is not to mention such terrifying revelations as the Michael-Jackson-is-still-alive theory, or the true whereabouts of the passengers aboard doomed Paris-bound Flight AF447 in May 2009. Read on…

9/11

The War on Terror is said to have begun on 11 September 2001. But is it possible that the war began before this date? Some people point to US government complicity in the events of 9/11, either by not doing enough to prevent it, or – more ominously – by actively planning for it. Whatever the truth may be, there is plenty of conjecture that what happened on that day doesn't add up to the popular version of the events. In fact, there is even a name for the loosely affiliated individuals and organizations dedicated to probing the official line: the 9/11 Truth Movement, which persists to this day in calling for a renewed investigation into the attacks.

What is not in dispute is that public support for the War on Terror was far greater after these attacks than it would have been on 10 September 2001. Could it be that the attacks were allowed to happen to create public clamour for a war which would otherwise have been inconceivable? Many people have pointed to the possibility that the events of 9/11 clone those of Pearl Harbor, an attack on the US naval base which, according to some, US officials deliberately allowed to take place in order to further the war aims of President Roosevelt. But a more sinister comparison has been made by those sceptical of the motives of the George W. Bush administration. They claim that what happened was more akin to Adolf Hitler's burning of the Reichstag, the German Republic's parliament building, on 27 February 1933. Hitler blamed the fire on communists plotting against the state, but historians widely accept the view that a member of the Prussian Interior Ministry set fire to the building deliberately – on Hitler's orders. Immediately after the fire, Hitler announced an emergency decree which suspended the normal civil rights and liberties of citizens and gave the government complete autonomy. This was the beginning of the end for German democratic values and heralded the rise of the Nazi dictatorship.

In October 2001 Congress approved Bush's Patriot Act, a bill which reduced the civil liberties of US citizens and allowed the detention without trial of anyone the government deemed a potential "security threat". Furthermore, the public and political pressure for retaliation for the attacks was intense, and neatly tied into the agenda of the "Project for a New American Century". This was a strategic document put forward by a group of neoconservatives in September 2000, outlining a new approach for US global dominance in the twenty-first century. This think tank included Dick Cheney, the vice president; Donald Rumsfeld, the secretary of defense; Paul Wolfowitz, his deputy; Jeb Bush, brother of George W. and governor of Florida; and Lewis Libby, the leader of Bush's 2000 election campaign team who was then working in the White House.

The most intriguing part of the document concerns the readjustment of US military forces across the globe. The report states that only an incremental approach can be taken to this radical restructuring owing to political and public constraints, unless there happened to be "some catastrophic and catalysing event like a new Pearl Harbor".

Despite all this, however, there is still the question of how such an elaborate attack could have been prepared and executed by the government and its agencies without the media becoming deeply suspicious. The most likely explanation is that the attacks were planned by Osama bin Laden and al-Qaeda but that US intelligence agencies did not act upon the information they received to adequately prevent them. Evidence of their failure of prevention, whether deliberate or through incompetence, has been widespread following congressional investigations but without any "smoking gun". Then again, the CIA and New York City counterterrorism offices were based in Building 7 of the World Trade Center and were therefore destroyed, along with any potentially incriminating evidence.

The suspicions about intelligence are just part of the mistrust about the events that day, which reverberated right around the world in the atrocity's aftermath. On the day of the attacks, geological surveys in New York recorded the greatest amount of seismic activity occurring immediately before the Twin Towers collapsed, and not when they hit the ground. This led many people to the conclusion that the towers were blown up with explosives planted directly underneath the buildings and not by the enormous volume of fuel that ignited after the two airliners exploded; a belief reinforced by the way the towers imploded instead of collapsing sideways.

John Farmer, the former attorney general of New Jersey and senior counsel for the 9/11 Commission, has released a book entitled *The Ground Truth*. Farmer claims that the official version of events is based on false testimony and documents and is largely untrue. He says "at some level of the government, at some point in time… there was an agreement not to tell the truth about what happened… The [NORAD – North American Aerospace Defense Command] tapes told a radically different story from what had been told to us and the public for two years. This is not spin." His sentiments appear confirmed by the 9/11 Commission head, Thomas Kean: "We to this day don't know why NORAD told us what they told us, it was just so far from the truth…" However, neither Kean nor Farmer offer any alternative explanation for 9/11, let alone who was behind it, and the statements are lost in the vortex of mystery surrounding these events.

The evidence at the Pentagon also raises troubling questions. Why was the Pentagon hit on the one side of the building that happened to be empty on the day of the attacks, owing to refurbishment? Why was there no visible evidence of a destroyed airliner among the debris? Why were no fighter jets scrambled to intercept the hijacked aircraft until after the third plane had hit the Pentagon, despite it being a legal requirement in the US for fighter jets to be scrambled whenever a commercial airliner veers significantly off its flight path? How was so much information known about the hijackers and released to the media by the FBI so soon after the attacks, including details on a passport miraculously found among the rubble of the Twin Towers? Why are at least six of the supposed hijackers still alive? And how can it be that the flight manifests, released publicly, contain no Arab names?

The fate of the fourth plane, United Airlines flight 93, has also caused controversy – this airliner crashed in a field near Shanksville, Pennsylvania, after the passengers revolted. It was the only plane out of the four to miss its target. A popular theory suggests that it was in fact shot down by a US fighter jet. Why? Because the passengers had found out the truth about the plot and had successfully intervened – the government could not allow there to be any survivors who could point the finger at them.

These questions raise serious doubts about the official version of what happened on 11 September 2001. Aside from these troubling claims, the events of 9/11 have given rise to a plethora of other, more bizarre, related theories. For example, the Wingdings conspiracy purports that even Microsoft were involved on some level. By selecting the font "Wingdings" in Microsoft Word and entering "q33ny", a plane, two buildings, a skull and crossbones, and a Star of David appear. Advocates of this theory maintain that "q33ny" was a flight number of one of the hijacked planes. It wasn't. The theory persists, however, and some go so far as to read anti-Semitic messages regarding New York City into this. By entering "NYC" into the Wingdings font, a skull and crossbones, the Star of David and a thumbs-up icon appear, which theory proponents take as a subliminal message to kill the Jews of New York.

David Icke would have us believe that reptilian shape-shifting aliens, who control the entire world's governing bodies, were to blame. Whatever the truth, the dust from the events of that fateful day show no signs of settling anytime soon.

ADOLF HITLER

Although the accepted account is that Adolf Hitler killed himself, along with his wife Eva Braun, at the end of World War Two, recent tests on what was supposed to have been his skull showed it to be that of a woman instead. So could that mean he survived after all? There are several different theories about where Hitler could have gone.

Some say that he escaped to Argentina, along with Nazi officers responsible for the Holocaust, taking the Nazis' supplies of stolen gold with him. The theory is that he managed to get on to a U-boat, which then sailed across the Atlantic and secretly deposited the dictator before surrendering itself to the Argentinian authorities.

Others agree that he used a U-boat to escape but think his location of choice was a little colder. As early as 1939, a secret German expedition was made to part of Antarctica with the intention of building a base there. Some think that the U-boat dropped Hitler off at the completed base in 1945 – or possibly even before the end of the war, with body doubles taking his place in Germany to avoid suspicion – before continuing to

Argentina to surrender. Later, British SAS soldiers were linked with operations in the area and, in the following few years until the early 1950s, US forces were reported to have violently attacked Antarctica in secret, using atomic weapons on several occasions. Some believe that the British and US forces were trying to kill Hitler and destroy his secret base, although no one knows if they were successful.

A third theory suggests that Hitler may have escaped to the moon. The Nazis had been developing complex and sophisticated weapons for several years before the end of the war, including rockets. Some think that one of these rockets was used to take the Führer into space to live in a secret colony on the moon – some even think that there are up to 40,000 people living in the colony, which has been kept secret from the rest of the world to provide a secure living space for the world's elite. The theory has it that the atmosphere on the moon is breathable, and that Hitler would have no problem living out his life in comfort and safety there.

We may never know what really happened to Hitler in 1945, but one thing is certain: even if he did survive the war, it is likely that he would have died by now – he would have celebrated his 130th birthday in 2019.

AIDS

AIDS was quite possibly one of the most horrific developments of the twentieth century. Millions of pounds have been poured into research yet a cure still seems all but elusive. Gone are the days of carefree sex 'n' drugs 'n' rock 'n' roll; the deadly virus isn't at all discriminatory about who it infects.

Shocking as the whole phenomenon would be if this really was a natural plague, theory has it that the AIDS virus was in fact artificially manufactured by the US government to kill off the so-called "useless eaters" of the human race: blacks, homosexuals and drug users, to be more precise. The Minister of Health for Louis Farrakhan's Nation of Islam, Dr Abdul Alim Muhammad, called for a formal investigation. In his words: "We know from the Congressional Report that money was appropriated for the creation of artificial biological agents to defeat the immune system. This took place in July of 1969. Ten million dollars was allocated to the US Army. So... let there be hearings to uncover the files."

In an experiment that took place in Tuskegee, Alabama, from 1932 to 1972, about 400 poor black men were used as guinea pigs as scientists studied the effects of syphilis left untreated. This experiment caused much distrust among African Americans, leading many to suspect the government of intentionally introducing the AIDS virus into the black community via such medical trials.

Over 30 years later, a study by Rand Corp found that 16 per cent of African Americans believed AIDS was created to reduce the black population, while 25 per cent believed it was manufactured in a laboratory. No doubt the notion arose because the disease was initially found in homosexuals and African Americans. The theory postulates that the US Special Cancer Virus Program (SCVP) is responsible for creating the disease, and that it was then spread among the population with the smallpox vaccination, or to gay men with the hepatitis B vaccination.

Other anti-black conspiracy theories include: that Charles Drew, the black Washington physician whose pioneering work with blood plasma saved thousands of lives, died after a car accident because he was denied entry into a whites-only hospital; that Tropical Fantasy, a soft drink produced by a firm employing large numbers of ethnic minorities, was actually a product of the Ku Klux Klan and contained chemicals to sterilize black men, and there have been similar allegations about Church's Chicken chain and Snapple soft drinks.

An outspoken critic of the HIV/AIDS link is Peter Duesberg, who claims that HIV is not a virus at all and has no bearing on the onset of AIDS. He maintains that non-infectious agents such as sexual intercourse and drug taking – both recreational and pharmaceutical – are the true causes of AIDS.

We cannot know the origins of AIDS. We do not know whether the most lethal worldwide killer was born of some warped conspiracy in the name of population control or scientific experiment, but "they" definitely succeeded if a conspiracy was at work – perhaps they had not bargained for such dramatic results.

ALEXANDER LITVINENKO

When former Russian Secret Service officer Alexander Litvinenko died on 23 November 2006 in a London hospital, the cause of death was determined as the first recorded case of polonium-210-induced acute radiation syndrome. But the question of who was responsible still hangs in the air.

The most popular theory is that the Russian government was behind the death of one of its old boys, not least because it was President Vladimir Putin that Litvinenko openly accused of poisoning him. In a letter written on his deathbed and published in the UK media shortly after his demise, Litvinenko claimed that the Russian head of state was the "person responsible for my present condition", before going on to accuse him of being "barbaric and ruthless [...] unworthy of your office [and] of the trust of civilized men and women." This theory has since been endorsed (though not proved) by official sources. In *The Litvinenko Inquiry*, published in 2016, Sir Robert Owen wrote, "Taking full account of all the evidence and analysis available to me, I find that the FSB operation to kill Litvinenko was probably approved by Mr Patrushev and also by President Putin."

CONSPIRACY THEORIES

Litvinenko had fled to the West to escape persecution at home and had become a harsh critic of the conduct of the Russian state, and in particular the Putin regime, authoring two incendiary books (*Blowing up Russia: The Secret Plot to Bring Back KGB Terror* and *Lubyanka Criminal Group*). He linked the government to various acts of terrorism, including the Moscow apartment bombings in 1999.

He was also very outspoken in his support for those who found themselves in conflict with the Russian government, metaphorically and literally, such as the murdered journalist Anna Politkovskaya and various Chechen rebel figures. So it is easy to see why Putin would have wanted him silenced.

It is claimed that Litvinenko was slipped the deadly dose in a drink at the Pine Bar at the Millennium Hotel, Grosvenor Square, during a meeting with Andrei Lugovi and Dmitry Kovtun, two former Russian intelligence men. Lugovi is the man thought to be the mastermind of the operation. People opposed to the consumption of raw fish were quick to say that the poisoning took place at the itsu sushi bar in Piccadilly – the sushi chain was subsequently hit by a drop in sales. Litvinenko fell ill the same day (1 November) and died just over three weeks later.

The British police discovered polonium trails across London linked both to Litvinenko, Lugovi and Kovtun, including in the office of another Russian political refugee, billionaire businessman Boris Berezovsky, and on British Airways' aircraft that had travelled between London and Moscow prior to and following the poisoning. An extradition request for Lugovi was denied.

Putin's government is not the only accused in the case of the poisoning of Alexander Litvinenko. Many believe that the involvement of the shady figure of Boris Berezovsky, reportedly an anti-Putin ally, was more sinister. Polonium trails evidence suggested that he was acquainted with Lugovi, Kovtun and Litvinenko.

Berezovsky was also a fierce critic of the Putin administration and it is claimed that he helped engineer the death of fellow dissident Litvinenko in an attempt to besmirch the president and bring down the Russian government.

Another theory has it that it was enemies made by Litvinenko during his time at the organized crime department of the FSB (the successor of the KGB) who orchestrated the killing as a means of silencing the increasingly talkative former state employee.

Other sources say that it was the British government that despatched Litvinenko. It is rumoured that the ex-FSB man was a British spy whose usefulness had come to an end and whose volatility had become a risk too big to ignore.

ALIEN BIG CATS

Stories of mysterious feline creatures being sighted on an English moor, in a Scottish glen or in a Welsh valley are becoming as commonplace as reports on corrupt politicians. Many people claim to have spotted a gigantic beast roaming the wilds, its threatening shadow recognizable as that of a cat of unnatural proportions. So, what exactly is out there?

According to one theory, these animals are alien big cats; not unworldly life forms as their name suggests, but of earthly origin. They are the original discarded creatures from circuses, illegally imported collections, zoos and other travelling shows. They are panthers, pumas, lynxes, caracals, ocelots, tigers, cougars and jungle cats which have been abandoned to the wild and have joined the feral population. Some believe that the cats that stalk the remote countryside are hybrids; abandoned wild cats that have found a new home in sparsely populated rural areas, where they have bred with indigenous creatures, producing new species. This would explain the abnormal size and form, and suggests they are the product of a natural process of evolution.

However, could these felines be undiscovered exotic breeds which have always existed in isolated numbers, feeding off unattended livestock?

The number of sightings has increased from a handful in the hills and mountains of Europe, the US and Australia in the 1950s to much more frequent discoveries today. The Beast of Bodmin Moor, the Blue Mountains Panther and the Tantanoola Tiger are no longer unusual tales of mystery and magic. Is this increase explainable by the introduction of tougher animal welfare laws that have forced unscrupulous owners to desert their once-prized possessions? Maybe.

But what should be made of suggestions that these alien big cats are able to disappear, that they are bulletproof, and are capable of leaping impossible heights and distances and altering their form? How can the eyes that burn like bright red bulbs be explained? Are these big cats really alien? Have extraterrestrials come to our planet and disguised themselves as giant felines so that they can secretly stalk the globe and gather information on its inhabitants, possibly ahead of an all-out attack on us?

ALIENS

It has yet to be proved categorically whether aliens exist, but reported sightings and abductions have certainly led to a whole minefield of speculation about why the government and powers that be might want to hide their existence from us and what the aliens' intentions toward us might be.

What is perhaps most disturbing is the suggestion that the Western world's leaders are heavily involved with the aliens. This involvement would appear first and foremost to be military. Witnesses testify to the fact that particularly high numbers of UFOs are spotted around military bases worldwide, and that there are military centres hidden underground all over the US. What could the US government be trying to hide? There is the theory that aliens either visit, or are kept in, Area 51 – a rumour that has been in circulation since the infamous Roswell incident of 1947.

The period January–September 2009 saw more UFO reports than any previous full-year period since records began in 1997. One such report was filed by a pilot flying over Oxfordshire who saw a flying disc about 60 metres above him. The report was forwarded on to the UFO Desk by air traffic controllers, possibly from RAF station Brize Norton, with a Ministry of Defence spokesman confirming that most reports do originate from there.

Of course, not all reports are from the military, and in 1962 a 14-year-old named Alex Birch photographed what appeared to be a whole group of flying saucers. His sci-fi fantasy was dashed when the Air Ministry concluded that the photo depicted not UFOs but reflections of sunlight from ice crystals, giving the impression of flying saucers in the smoky atmosphere. It would seem from their response that the Air Ministry was only too keen to come up with a "logical" explanation that ruled out the possibility of any extraterrestrial visitation.

Aliens are sometimes presented as harmless, rather clueless little green men, but the testimonies of those who claim to have been abducted by aliens and rendered powerless to protect themselves from various assaults suggest that perhaps the intentions of extraterrestrial beings are not entirely laudable.

In the famous case of Barney and Betty Hill in 1961, who reported a time loss of two hours after spotting a UFO in the night skies over New Hampshire, subsequent hypnosis revealed that the couple appeared to have not only been abducted by aliens, but to have also undergone physical and mental tests. They both gave a clear description of what is now the archetypal alien depiction – big grey head, slanted eyes. After six months of hypnotherapy, the therapist, Dr Simon, released his expert opinion that Betty and Barney had indeed been abducted and taken aboard a spacecraft. In the following years, the Hills spent time with numerous researchers and scientists, not one of whom dispelled the notion of abduction.

Of course, we cannot know for sure that the accounts of the Hills and numerous other alleged alien abductees are solid evidence of interactions with aliens. But the possibility that governments and the military could make a deal with an alien race is not inconceivable. After all, why not allow these foreign races to take animals and humans for experiments, genetic engineering or any other purpose in exchange for technology far beyond our own primitive scientific knowledge? And let's face facts: the technology required to efficiently cross galaxies would eclipse anything we have yet conceived, and all governments would want to get their hands on it. Stories of abductions would suggest that aliens and those who deal with them have proved themselves to be far from trustworthy. Such actions are frightening and point to nothing less than a malevolent conspiracy.

Maybe the aliens trick our governments by using the guise of exploration. By pretending to have no intention of domination, extraterrestrials could be visiting our planet at this very moment, studying the human race for possible future invasion. It would seem that the fate of our entire race, not to mention our planet, is at stake here. World domination by an extraterrestrial people is not an entirely comfortable prospect.

However, most reported UFO sightings don't record any contact with aliens; perhaps we can conclude from this that if aliens are visiting the planet, they're not all interested in conducting tests and experiments. On the other hand, maybe they're not interested in testing us at all; perhaps they're just stopping to ask for directions?

AREA 51

For many years there has been speculation about what really takes place in a remote part of the Nevada desert near Roswell, New Mexico, that has come to be known as Area 51. A former airfield which, in 1955, was turned into a top-secret site for developing spy planes, has become infamous for its secrecy and strange goings-on. Even the airfield's name wasn't recognized by the US government until 2013, and it seems certain that something is taking place there which the public is not meant to know about.

The official line suggests that the area is a military testing facility. The only concrete information we have is geographical – we know that it is to the north of Las Vegas. Beyond that, we enter into a whole web of cover-up and conspiracy. Few people know what really goes on there. Curtained off by a no-fly zone which extends all the way up to space, it seems impossible to glean any reliable information. The military appears to go to quite excessive measures to prevent any hope of entry. If the area is a military firing range, this is justifiable, but still, the entry prohibitions seem stringent to say the least. The area is fenced off, the fence being guarded by hundreds of closed-circuit security cameras worthy of a modern-day Berlin Wall. Signs in the proximity warn that deadly force and violence are quite permissible to prevent intruders. Someone seems very keen to keep people out. The roads surrounding the area are guarded by camouflaged vehicles bearing government plates. They are manned by men who wear military-style desert uniforms and are armed with M16 rifles. Moreover, the roads are full of sensors which transmit any vehicle movement on the roads. All this does not seem to point to a conventional military base.

Now that the spy planes have been developed and moved from Area 51, it is not known what the area is used for today. All we know is that there is a large airbase which is not recorded on any map. Some intrepid explorers have risked their lives by photographing it from nearby hills, and a few photographs taken by Russian and commercial satellites are now available – including a picture of a recently built hangar, which disproves theories that Area 51 has been closed by the government.

One theory would have it that the area is a research centre for investigating UFOs and for manufacturing the infamous black helicopters. Certainly, UFOs would need to be taken somewhere for investigation, such as in the aftermath of the Roswell incident of 1947, when the wreckage of what was rumoured to have been a flying saucer was recovered from a ranch in New Mexico. Of course, the US government could also be trying to reproduce the technology gleaned from the alien spacecraft here.

An even more disturbing and outlandish theory adhered to by some is that there are extraterrestrials being kept alive in the area, retrieved from their spacecraft. Who knows what could have happened to any aliens left behind in the aftermath of the alleged UFO crash at Roswell? If this is the case, it would seem that the authorities are sitting on a time bomb. Had any aliens managed to come to this planet, it would suggest that their technology is far superior to ours. Were they to be kept alive at Area 51, the possibility of them escaping confinement cannot be ruled out – and the consequences of such an event could be potentially catastrophic.

BARACK OBAMA

On 5 November 2008 a momentous event in US history occurred: Barack Obama defeated John McCain to become the 44th president of the US, and the country's first black leader. George W. Bush and his controversial Republican administration were defeated. But how did Obama get there?

Some believe that far-from-wholesome influences lay behind his ascendancy, which, from a childhood in Hawaii and Indonesia, encompassed education at Columbia University and Harvard Law School, 12 years as a civil rights attorney and three terms in the Illinois Senate (1997–2004), before his election as the leader of the free world.

Theorists claim that Obama's rise to power was a socialist conspiracy, orchestrated by a shadowy group of Jewish financiers linked to the powerful Rothschild dynasty. A Jewish businessman by the name of George Soros is allegedly the mastermind behind Obama's success. A life-long supporter of liberal causes, and bankrolled by the Rothschilds, Soros is said to have helped steer the Honolulu-born politician through a shining career to the presidency, even supposedly handpicking him to challenge Hillary Clinton in the Democratic Party leadership contest and subsequently the Republican presidential candidate McCain. Obama's efforts to radically reform the US healthcare system, which have met with fierce opposition from the corporate and Christian right, are seen by some as evidence of the hand of socialism in his elevation and policy making.

Others suggest that Obama owes his position to the support of the Kennedy family. Speculation goes that it was John F. Kennedy who helped Obama's father come to the US from Kenya and receive an expensive university education. From this secure base he was able to launch his son on a journey that would take him from America's newest state to 1600 Pennsylvania Avenue, Washington, and the US presidency.

The influence of another prominent US clan has also been speculated upon: the Nation of Islam. There are people who believe Obama is the illegitimate son of Malcolm X, former leader of the organization, and that his supporters in the Nation of Islam have helped guide him to become the first African American to take power in the White House. Can Obama's desire for universal healthcare be linked to this clandestine support? To which ethnic group do the vast majority of US citizens without healthcare coverage belong? Are they not black men, women and children?

A further theory to develop during Obama's presidency was that he was trying to bankrupt the US as he hated the country and wanted to destroy it from within. This is despite the fact that he was elected to his first term after the start of the global economic recession that began in 2007. The evidence at hand is that Obama failed to decrease the US financial deficit during his time in office – it actually grew, though most of the money was owed to concerns within the US itself. No matter why or how, this failure is seen by many theorists as malicious, a popular line of reasoning being that Obama is secretly a Muslim extremist, thus explaining his concealed hatred of the country he led.

BENAZIR BHUTTO

The assassination of former Pakistani Prime Minister Benazir Bhutto on 27 December 2007 in Rawalpindi as she campaigned as leader of the opposition Pakistan People's Party (PPP) has become another chapter in the Kafkaesque story of Pakistani politics. Conspiracy theories abound with regards to who was responsible for this crime.

The finger has been pointed by many at General Pervez Musharraf, president of Pakistan at the time. He took the position following a military coup in 1999 and held it until he was forced, under impeachment, to resign in August 2008.

The return of Bhutto to Pakistan after years of exile was an obvious threat to Musharraf's power and financial base. The pro-Musharraf Pakistan Muslim League Party (PML-Q) was facing defeat in the general election and it is said that Bhutto had agreed a deal with the then president that would see his role diminish. In the heated world of Pakistani politics, Musharraf faced an undignified loss of control.

Al-Qaeda claimed responsibility for the assassination but this admission far from absolves Musharraf and his regime.

The man and his cronies were widely linked with extremist groups, and it is claimed that he used them as covert armed forces to quell dissent in a highly fractious political environment. If this is true, obtaining the services of a rogue element within al-Qaeda or the Taliban would have been an option for the president.

Musharraf may not even have had to outsource to militants. The Inter-Services Intelligence (ISI) agency has reportedly been used by numerous Pakistani prime ministers to suppress political opposition and would have been more than capable of targeting Bhutto in a domestic setting. Just like Musharraf, the ISI and the army would have faced a drastic loss of power if Bhutto had been able to contest and win the election.

The ease with which the gunman and suicide bomber were able to approach Bhutto's bullet- and bombproof Toyota Land Cruiser suggests some form of security services collusion. The security detail's negligence in allowing such access is highly suspicious considering she had survived a similar attack only a few months earlier in Karachi. That bombing claimed the lives of at least 139 people, many of whom were members of Bhutto's PPP.

Furthermore, according to an Israeli paper, the Pakistani government had blocked Bhutto's attempts to hire private security from the US and the UK, denying visas to foreign security contractors. Musharraf responded to the criticism over security by claiming that Bhutto's own recklessness had been to blame and that she had spent too long at the rally.

The confusion surrounding the cause of Bhutto's death has only served to heighten suspicion over alleged state involvement in the killing. Following the assassination, the Interior Ministry claimed she had died from a fractured skull sustained from hitting her head against the sunroof handle in her car, thus contradicting local hospital reports.

Her opponents' assertion that her death was in some way accidental could easily be interpreted as an attempt to lessen her status as a martyr and hence the potency of the impact of her demise on her party's chances in the forthcoming election.

Musharraf is not the only suspect, however. There is speculation that Prime Minister Nawaz Sharif ordered the killing. The two figures were bitter political enemies and there is a long-running enmity between Sharif and the Bhutto family, with the Lahore-born politician responsible for the arrest of Bhutto's husband on charges of corruption. He spent over a decade in jail as a result.

There have also been allegations that the US government had some involvement. The theory goes that, even though they had backed Bhutto's risky return from exile, they collaborated in her assassination in order to expedite the fall of Musharraf from power. His supposedly clandestine support for extremist groups on the Pakistan and Afghanistan border had become a major barrier to the success of the US's War on Terror.

BIG BROTHER IS WATCHING YOU

Do you ever feel that THEY are watching you? Have you ever wondered if you are in the hands of the authorities, the plaything of a conspiracy about which you know nothing and over which you have no control? The world of George Orwell's *1984* does not seem so far off when you consider the following:

- Surveillance devices now in the hands of government officials include, according to Massachusetts Institute of Technology (MIT) professor Gary Marx, "heat-sensing imaging devices that can tell if a house is occupied, voice amplifiers, light amplifiers, night-vision devices and techniques for reading mail without breaking the seal." Cameras can be concealed in virtually any piece of furniture and police can use listening devices or phone records to track the conversations of anyone they suspect of being involved in crime.

- On a typical day, thousands of telephone calls are legally recorded by authorities. How many calls are being eavesdropped on illegally? In some countries, every international phone call may be recorded and monitored. Monitoring domestic calls is sometimes illegal, but the development of technology means that a huge number of long-distance phone calls can now be intercepted and recorded (whether legally or illegally).

- Police routinely take DNA from anyone arrested for an offence other than littering or parking infringements. The world's largest DNA databases are in China (estimated at more than 8 million individuals, less than 1 per cent of the population), the USA (14.3 million, around 4.5 per cent of the population) and the UK (5.6 million, about 9 per cent of the population).

- The US has the world's most extensive system of computer databases of personal information on civilians. The information is collected for purposes ranging from monitoring criminals to credit reporting and market research. The types of personal information collected include the impersonal basics, such as names and addresses, but may also completely invade an individual's privacy by storing such information as medical records, psychological profiles, drinking habits, and political and religious beliefs. A new government project, the Homeland Advanced Recognition Technology (HART) system, will record a wider range of biometric data such as iris scans, palm prints, voice patterns, scars, tattoos and even DNA, which will be linked to names, addresses, number plates and any other information officials can add to make a record of every individual the system comes into contact with.

- Electronic espionage has now become so common that few people even see it as a problem. Networking software packages have worker-monitoring features built in as a matter of course, which can now record an employee's every activity and store it for later analysis or send automated messages to someone's computer telling them to work faster. "Look in on Sue's computer screen," exhorts one ad for a major networking package. "Sue doesn't even know you're there!"

- According to a US government study, the FBI's database of criminal histories is totally incomplete and inaccurate. Thousands of citizens are at risk of false arrest because of this.

- It is a policy of the US Navy to collect DNA samples from all new recruits. Who knows how long it will be before they start genetically engineering perfect sailors?

- US Customs and Border Protection has a computer system that classifies incoming airline passengers as "high risk" or "low risk" based on Passenger Name Record (PNR) data supplied by the airlines. The purpose is supposedly to speed up lines at customs counters. "Americans are meant to be free people. There's not supposed to be records made when you travel," said a sceptical US congressman. "The minute you get your name and birth date into a computer in Washington, watch out."

- In a more recent development, it turns out that even our technology is keeping tabs on us. Aside from the "personalized" ads we see on the internet and the recommendations made by sites like Amazon – which have become a part of daily life for many people – there is something more sinister happening. Research has shown that apps downloaded to mobile devices are transmitting data which is collected for a number of purposes, mainly building a personal profile for marketing. They're accessing personal information and sharing it with companies, with implied consent due to the download – and they may be doing some of this even when the devices are believed to be switched off.

- Smartphones are believed to be weak spots when it comes to safeguarding our personal data. Some people believe that charging a device in a public wall socket can result in stolen data, while others claim that the stickers attached to mobile phone batteries are used for covert data collection and transmission (in fact, they are merely Near Field Communication (NFC) transmitters and removing these stickers would render the device useless for apps using NFC such as Apple Pay and Google Wallet).

- New technologies designed to make people's lives easier are actually spying on them. Samsung's Smart TV, for example, is voice activated and simple to use, even making viewing suggestions. According to the marketing, it understands all accents. However, one thing that wasn't made clear to early adopters of this technology is that these TVs are *always* listening – again, even when they're switched off! The TVs "hear" everything that is said and send the data back to the manufacturers and interested parties. The TVs can even share the names of files on USB sticks inserted into them. Samsung have gone to the effort of alerting users to this issue, due to the outrage when the general public found out, but many other household items are heading in the same direction. Amazon Echo and other voice-activated assistants take things even further. Their primary function is to listen to what you say and to learn about you – so they can help you manage your life, of course. A study by Northeastern University noted that these smart speakers accidentally activate up to 19 times a day, recording as much as 43 seconds of audio each time. At this rate, even our washing machines could soon be acting as spies within our homes.

- Personal data is gathered by tech giants such as Facebook and is stored by users in cloud services by providers such as Google, Amazon, Microsoft and IBM. But what do they really do with the information once they get their hands on it, and is it really as private as you think it is?

BILL CLINTON

Many people have conjectured that former US President Bill Clinton is not what he appears to be. Some have gone so far as to question whether he is even human and have speculated that he is an extraterrestrial. Another theory suggests that he is neither human nor alien; it alleges that he has been manufactured and patented, and is actually a robot operated jointly by the FBI and a certain famous cartoon company.

But how do these theorists explain how he has been able to get away with it for so long? They would argue that it is only an indication of the superiority of current technology that he appears almost identical to a human and, what is more, is able to fool people in everyday situations. He can, for example, communicate with others on his own. During his presidency his foreign policies were resolved by his creators, as were his domestic programmes.

Clinton's notorious sexual escapades certainly help to make him seem all the more human – perhaps they were an intentional ploy on the part of the robot's creators? Some would say that the choice of Al Gore as his vice president served to make Clinton look positively superhuman.

CONSPIRACY THEORIES

Some right-wing groups are said to have become aware of the robotic nature of the former president when he was in power. But their theory was so bizarre that they were reluctant to go public and risk their own heads, so they set about bringing him down by more conventional means.

BLACK HELICOPTERS

On 7 May 1994, a black helicopter pursued a teenage boy for 45 minutes in Harahan, Louisiana. Its exterior gave nothing away, bearing no mark of its origin or owners. The boy was terrified not so much by the sinister nature of the vehicle itself, but by the threatening stance of its occupants, who had descended from the aircraft and aimed their weapons at him. The boy never discovered why the helicopter had targeted him. The police chief for the area was not forthcoming, intimating that the helicopters belonged to the US government and that the matter was completely out of his hands.

A week later, some people travelling in a car near Washington DC had a similar experience. They too were chased – with a black helicopter following their car for several miles. They were completely powerless; when the driver tried to escape from the road, a rope ladder dropped from the helicopter and men in black uniforms carrying weapons started to descend to the ground. There was no option but to do as the men in the aircraft wanted. The driver counts himself lucky that the volume of traffic forced the aircraft to retreat in the end, but does not wish to think what would have happened to him or his passengers if the road had been deserted.

Then in 1995, a black helicopter flew over a couple's farm in Nevada and sprayed an unknown substance over the area. This is believed to have resulted in the sudden death of more than a dozen of their animals along with extensive damage to surrounding vegetation. Official authorities denied any knowledge of the helicopter. The spraying of both urban and rural settings with unknown chemicals, and the killing of pets, plants and livestock for no apparent reason, is more ominous still.

Mysterious black helicopters seem to be constantly in evidence, pursuing and terrifying completely innocent victims. They have also been linked with a number of cases of cattle mutilation over the years, as these mysterious aircraft have been seen in immediate proximity before, during or after this bizarre crime has taken place. What is most alarming is that the occupants of the helicopters do not even pretend to have peaceable intentions and are quite prepared to use gunfire and other violent means to their advantage, all the time keeping their identities secret.

In March 1999 there were several sightings of mysterious black helicopters reported around the Pittsburgh area, many within the space of half an hour. One helicopter was seen to hover over the same residential street for around five minutes before leaving. Incredibly, it returned every day for the next three weeks and did the same thing each time. No explanation has ever been given for its actions.

Photos have been taken of unmarked black helicopters repeatedly performing unusual manoeuvres in residential areas – not over military land, as you might expect of a helicopter on a training exercise. Are the helicopters linked to the mysterious Men in Black? People who have dared to photograph the helicopters have allegedly been accosted by men wearing black uniforms. They have then been told to leave the area and have been forbidden to tell anyone what has happened. The men have also confiscated their cameras and film.

Whether the mysterious helicopters and their occupants are an alien phenomenon, or whether they are in fact from hostile government departments, we may never know. But it seems certain that they do not come in peace and that they are not prepared to uphold fundamental democratic principles and civil rights.

THE BOXING DAY TSUNAMI

On 26 December 2004, a devastating tsunami struck South East Asia. Waves of up to 30 metres hit the Indian Ocean coastline, killing almost 230,000 people. The Boxing Day tsunami is considered to be one of the deadliest natural disasters in modern times. However, some believe something more sinister lay behind the event.

One theory is that the US government was responsible for the tsunami, triggering it by detonating a nuclear bomb. Why did they do it? Oil. A natural disaster was created in order to take control of the oil reserves in the Aceh province of Indonesia. Having used direct intervention to bolster its oil supplies in Iraq, the Bush administration was confident that the same strategy would work again.

Early rescue worker reports, later supposedly destroyed, claimed that a force of 2,000 US marines arrived in the Aceh province shortly after the tsunami struck with orders to facilitate partial autonomy from the Indonesian government for the oil-rich area. They also found water samples to be radioactive.

Another explanation is that the US government used their High Frequency Active Auroral Research Program (HAARP) to set off the tsunami. HAARP is a project, funded in part by the US Navy and US Air Force, to research the use of the ionosphere as a communication and surveillance tool, and it is rumoured that a weather modification weapons system has been simultaneously developed. It was this child of the US Star Wars arms era that is blamed by some for creating the so-called natural disaster.

Others believe that it was India, not the US, which lay behind the nuclear detonation that caused the tsunami. The Indian government, keen to maintain the upper hand over neighbour Pakistan at a time when tensions between the two countries were running high, tested a nuclear device in a region of the Indian Ocean known as the Five Belt, which was identified as the epicentre of the earthquake.

Some attribute the Indian government's actions to more sinister motives: the extermination of a large swathe of humankind. With a history of hostility toward Muslims, it wouldn't be a coincidence that they chose a predominantly Muslim region of South East Asia as their target.

BREXIT

The referendum on whether the United Kingdom should leave the European Union, held on 23 June 2016, was one of the most monumental votes in British political history, and the subsequent "Leave" result sent shockwaves around the world. Quickly dubbed "Brexit" by the media, the process of preparing to leave the EU and negotiate a withdrawal deal became a torturous affair that divided the UK. Almost inevitably, it gave rise to scores of conspiracy theories, some more well-founded than others. Here are just some of the theories relating to this divisive topic:

- The EU is believed to be on the path to creating a single European superstate – a cultureless, homogeneous polity to be ruled over by unelected officials in Brussels. This was a popular theory among some "Brexiteers". For proof, they looked to developments such as the European courts, the European anthem, the Euro single currency and speculation around the creation of a European army.

BREXIT

- Fake news was circulated on social media during the referendum campaign and there may have been Russian interference. There is likely some truth in this: the University of Edinburgh reportedly found over 400 Twitter accounts that were used as Russian propaganda tools. Facebook has also said that fake news was a problem at the time, though the company did not release any statistics.

- Voter-suppression tactics were allegedly used to prevent certain groups, including the young and British citizens living abroad, from voting in the referendum. Many younger voters were dismayed to find that the referendum vote date coincided with the Glastonbury festival, potentially keeping 175,000 (likely Remain voters) away from the polls. And Brits living abroad for longer than 15 years needed to have been registered to vote in the UK in the last 15 years and be eligible to vote in the general election, which denied many the right to vote in the referendum. Some of these ex-pats subsequently launched legal challenges to the ruling.

- The crashing of the electoral registration website in the final hours before the deadline to register to vote was claimed to have been deliberate and not due to a spike in registrations, as was reported.

- British intelligence service MI5 were said to have planned to change votes manually – hence the provision of pencils rather than pens in polling booths. People took to Twitter urging voters to take their own pens with them when they went to vote.

- Conservative MP Sarah Wollaston was accused of being a Remain plant. The MP was on the Leave side at the beginning of the campaign but switched to Remain midway, raising suspicions that it had been planned all along.

- The "Establishment" was said to be working behind the scenes to derail the Brexit process and keep the UK in the EU, and the chaotic negotiations were just a ruse to win support for a second referendum.

THE BRITISH GOVERNMENT MAKE IT RAIN

Cloud seeding is a meteorological technique where specific particles are dispersed into clouds in an attempt to change the type of precipitation that will fall, or indeed to make any precipitation fall. There is, however, a darker side to this science.

Theorists believe that the government uses cloud seeding for their own means, to affect the nation's mood in ways that will benefit them. This can be reasonably innocuous: for example, summer-festival-goers may feel that cloud seeding has been used to make sure the festival is rainy, so that people won't be too tempted to party all day and night, which could lead to them being unproductive back at their desks – or even absent – on Monday. Indeed, one could speculate that politically active bands, especially those who oppose the government, may be more heavily targeted. However, sometimes the claims are far stronger.

One particularly notable case is that of Lynmouth in Devon. In 1952, 90 million tons of water flooded the village, claiming the lives of 35 people and the homes of 430. While it was officially seen as a natural disaster or an act of God, theorists believe that rain-making experiments could have caused the flooding. According to estimates, the region of Devon where Lynmouth is situated received 252 times its normal rainfall during the flooding. Also, the flooding occurred within a week of rainfall experiments undertaken by the RAF. Though this may be a simple coincidence, it is certainly disturbing, and the truth about whether this disaster was natural or man-made may never be uncovered.

THE BRITISH ROYAL FAMILY ARE ALIENS

The British royal family are an eccentric bunch. Gaffes, scandals and acts of general oddness are all part and parcel of their aristocratic lives. Some of them are a little funny-looking too. Why is this? Is it because, as some would have us believe, they are reptilian shape-shifting aliens?

According to one theory, the Windsor family were all sheltering from a World War Two Luftwaffe bombing raid when a stray explosive hit their hideaway, killing them all. An alien spacecraft, which had been hovering above our planet since the death of Queen Victoria, took this opportunity to infiltrate humankind, and replaced them. It assumed their identities using shape-shifting powers.

It is claimed that Prince Philip is the real leader of the royal pack. His fascination with UFOs is no clandestine hobby. His subscription to several extraterrestrial quarterlies and alleged regular covert visits to areas where sightings have been reported and to secret crash sites enable him to pick up vital messages and check up on old extraterrestrial friends. He is supposedly scared of exposure and, by personally following up every UFO lead, he ensures that no information relating to his true form can leak out.

Prince Philip's position as the senior extraterrestrial family member has been questioned on occasion, although there is no doubting that he was one of the first royal aliens – the disguise is clearly an early model: just look at the size of the top of his head and his ears! (The forehead problem seems to have been improved upon but they still clearly have problems with the ears.) Some say that his uncle, Lord Louis Mountbatten, was the alien commander-in-chief and point to his use of UFO interest as a cover that was passed on to his next-in-command. The assassination of his earthly body by the IRA in 1979 forced the alien being back to the mother ship.

While some believe that the aliens' presence on this planet is benign – they are here to explore the planet and use their royal identities to visit places and events that are off-limits to most – others suggest that their purpose is more sinister.

These theorists, who include ex-Coventry City goalkeeper and former sports presenter David Icke (self-styled "Son of the Godhead"), claim that the British royal family are part of a reptilian shape-shifting alien conspiracy to take over the world. Their goal is to create a totalitarian One World State, ruled over by a master race of beings from outer space. George W. Bush is also a member: that pretzel-eating injury was no freak mishap; shape-shifting causes occasional injury to the human tissue.

Their refreshment of choice is allegedly human blood and they're not afraid of permanently silencing those who threaten to expose their real identity. Was Diana, Princess of Wales, killed by this alien force because she had discovered their secret? Long mystified by Charles' insistence on separate beds, even while dating and in marriage, an unplanned visit to her partner's bedroom in the night is said to have laid the truth bare, as it is during the hours of darkness that they return to alien form. From that moment on, some say, Diana's days were numbered.

BRUCE LEE

Bruce Lee, dressed in the traditional Chinese outfit he wore in the movie *Enter the Dragon*, was laid to rest in Lake View Cemetery in Seattle on 31 July 1973. But long before his sudden and tragic death at the age of 32, rumours were rife throughout Asia that he had been dead for months.

The official pronouncement was of "death by misadventure" but, according to one source, Hong Kong Triads killed Lee because he had refused to pay them protection money. Indeed, some believe that the Triads had managed to kill Lee using a pressure-point attack, which left him like a ticking time bomb – he would have felt fine directly after the attack, but his body would have been preparing to shut down. This is seen as the holy grail of martial arts: to be able to cause delayed death, with the simple use of pressure points.

Another source claimed that Lee had been drugged by a former sensei (teacher) who resented the fact that he taught martial arts to foreigners. Many Chinese people believe that Lee was the victim of his own rigorous training regime, while others cite drug abuse as the cause of his demise. It is even claimed by some cynics that Lee faked his death and that he is merely waiting for the right time to return to society.

The most popular story printed in the Hong Kong press suggested that the US Mafia had killed Lee. After completing *The Green Hornet*, Lee was approached by Mafia agents who wanted him to become the first Asian star in Hollywood. Bravely, Lee refused and went home to Hong Kong. In the aftermath, it is alleged that humiliated Mafia bosses signed Lee's death warrant and hired a professional assassin. An interesting postscript to this story claims that Lee's son, Brandon, also a martial arts actor, was "accidentally" shot dead after he found vital information about his father's killer. In 1993, Brandon died in mysterious circumstances while filming cult classic *The Crow*. In a scene where he was to be shot, in which there would usually be no bullet in the gun, a fatal mistake was made and Brandon was shot dead on set. There are many who believe his death was no accident at all and that it was murder, echoing the death of his father. Indeed, perhaps it was even the same culprits, not wanting Bruce Lee's son to survive and carry on his legacy.

Perhaps the most outrageous theory regarding Lee's death is that a prostitute killed him in a fit of panic. If the story is to be believed, Lee had taken a powerful aphrodisiac which had caused him to become very violent during sex. Fearing for her life, the prostitute reached out for the nearest heavy object – a glass ashtray – and struck Lee on the skull. He would never wake from the resulting coma.

Countless documentaries, books and magazines have purported to tell the "true" story of Bruce Lee's death. As far as the people of Hong Kong are concerned, the full facts surrounding Lee's passing have never been revealed, and probably never will be.

CALIFORNIA WILDFIRES

In the summer of 2018, a series of large wildfires devastated parts of California, leading to the declaration of a national disaster in Northern California. In November the same year, strong winds aggravated conditions in another round of state-wide destructive fires. These included the Camp Fire – which killed at least 85 people and destroyed more than 18,000 structures, becoming California's deadliest and most destructive wildfire on record – and the Mendocino Complex Fire, which burned more than 459,000 acres (186,000 hectares), the largest complex fire in the state's history.

Various factors were considered to have contributed to the severity of the 2018 California wildfire season, including an increase of natural fuel in the area, in the form of dead trees, along with compounding atmospheric conditions linked to global warming. But there was also another theory doing the rounds on Facebook forums, YouTube videos and Reddit threads: this theory stated that the fires were deliberately started by a secret cabal of influential billionaires, including Facebook's Mark Zuckerberg and Google's Sergey Brin, who are alleged to be linked to shadowy forces that seek to oppress the human race and run the world.

Proponents of the theory claim that "light pillars" from the sky were seen targeting rural homes. These deadly rays, capable of igniting fires hotter and faster-spreading than nature could ever produce, allegedly came from directed energy weapons (DEWs). And why would the operators of these weapons want to burn down these homes? To force the unsuspecting residents out of the rural areas and into cities, where they can be more easily controlled. Some have proposed that the fires were part of a plot to move people out of the way for construction of a transit system that would be key to an eventual state takeover. Proponents of these claims point to a map circulated online with the title "Wildfires line up EXACTLY in the same path as the California High Speed Rail System". (Sceptics have pointed out that the geography of the map is off, as it incorrectly shows that fires engulfed San Diego, Los Angeles, San Jose, San Francisco and Sacramento, and it does not line up with the train's proposed route.)

DEWs are in fact a real technology, though still in its infancy. A report produced for Congress described them as systems "that produce concentrated electromagnetic energy and atomic or subatomic particles". The idea is that laser beams could be used in combat for killing enemy troops and/or destroying enemy missiles, aircraft or satellites, though there are various logistical issues to surmount before that could work in practice on the battlefield. But those who argue that DEWs were involved in starting the wildfires would tell you that they are already operational and being used for nefarious purposes.

Believers of the DEW theory also claim that California's weather has been deliberately altered, or "geoengineered", to produce a parched landscape that made it that much easier for the fires to take hold. In addition, it's been claimed that aircraft have been dumping drying agents in the form of "chemtrails" to help dry out the landscape. "Chemtrails" is a word that conspiracy theorists use to refer to what they believe are the trails left behind by aircraft pumping out chemicals into the sky, which look the same as the harmless condensation, or contrails, generated by normal planes (for other theories surrounding the alleged purpose and effect of chemtrails, see page 65).

THE CHELYABINSK METEOR

In 2013, the world was shocked by footage of a huge meteor descending toward Russia and exploding in a massive ball of flame over the Chelyabinsk region. Stunned eyewitnesses stated that they could feel heat from the fireball. It was the sort of incredible natural phenomenon that people don't ever expect to see.

This phenomenon has inevitably led to theorists coming up with explanations for the meteor's unexpected appearance. The first was put forward by, among others, Gary C. Daniels, author of several texts on the Mayan prophecies. He argued that, although the date set in the Mayan calendar for the end of the world (2012) has passed, the natural disasters which have happened since are proof that the Mayan prophecies are true. The suggestion is that 21 December 2012 was the beginning of a new era of catastrophe, of which the meteor was part.

A second theory suggests that the lights in the sky were the result of a weapons test. Although a Russian news source claimed that the explosion had been caused by a Russian missile, some theorists believe that the entire event was actually an American weapons test.

Another two theories, on the weirder end of the spectrum, are that the event was the precursor to an alien invasion, or that we're all part of a conceptual computer game. Theorists believe that a video games developer managed the ultimate achievement in programming and created code that allows a game to manifest in reality.

Whatever the cause of the Chelyabinsk meteor, those who witnessed this event will certainly never forget it.

CHEMTRAILS

The chemical trails – or chemtrails – conspiracy claims that aircraft regularly spray harmful substances over the world's population for malicious purposes. The chemtrails appear in the sky in the same manner as the harmless condensation, or contrails, generated by normal planes, giving cover to their nefarious intent.

Many believe that the chemtrails technology is a product of the Star Wars weaponry era, instigated by the Reagan administration in the 1980s and now being used as a means to control the global population by a shadowy US-government-led cartel. Overpopulation is becoming an increasingly serious problem, with living space and natural resources dwindling fast. Chemtrails are a potential solution to this overcrowding. It is thought that the aircraft responsible for depositing the dangerous chemicals are the reason behind the occurrence of a rising number of particularly robust and life-threatening infectious diseases, such as the H1N1 and SARS viruses, which have allegedly been developed in secret laboratories.

Another part of this supposed plan is the preparation of national parks across the world to act as biospheres to perpetuate animal life ready for the new global dawn, at which point in time the human population will have been reduced to just a fraction of its twenty-first-century level.

Others speculate that chemtrails are being used by the corporate right to mask the impact of greenhouse gases on global warming. By burning sulphur in the stratosphere, a cool haze is created which has a positive short-term effect on the planet's temperature. This process, dubbed "global dimming", is allowing major polluting industries to continue their practices and maintain high-profit margins while at the same time suppressing more ecologically friendly alternatives.

Another theory is that chemtrails are part of an electromagnetic weather-conditioning weapon developed by the US government through its High Frequency Active Auroral Research Program (HAARP). Some say that the weapon has been used to further the interests of the oil industry and the figures within government that are connected to it.

It is claimed that chemtrails were part of a plan to trigger the Boxing Day tsunami in the Indian Ocean, the purpose of which was to gain access to the oil-rich Indonesian province of Aceh. It is rumoured that the same weapon was used to magnify the power of Hurricane Katrina, a storm which brought to a halt a large volume of domestic crude oil and gas production in the surrounding areas and thus allowed US oil companies to drive up their prices.

Theorists also suggest that chemtrails were connected to the Sichuan earthquake in China in 2008, a so-called natural disaster that seriously affected the world's fastest growing economy. Was the US government motivated by a deteriorating relationship with China over their own weakening position in the global trade hierarchy?

Some theorists believe that it is not the US government that was behind chemtrails, but that they are the work of a secretive New World Order that is engineering global destabilization in order to weaken global superpowers to an extent where they will be unable to halt the ascendancy of an all-powerful oil-based autocracy.

CHERNOBYL: WAS IT AN ACCIDENT?

What actually happened? Was it an accident? Or were there in fact ulterior motives behind a conscious experiment?

Over the years many people have wondered whether the huge explosion in reactor 4 at the Chernobyl nuclear power plant on 26 April 1986 happened because the reactor had purposefully been pushed into an extremely dangerous situation. The accident occurred when a scheduled experiment devised to eliminate certain safety issues went awry. A series of reported "mistakes" had occurred during the process leading up to the experiment. But why would the Soviet authorities have ordered such a large-scale disaster, devastating the lives of so many people?

The most widely suggested explanation is that the disaster constituted an experiment in preparation for fighting a nuclear war. If the Russian government was putting a plan for nuclear war against the West into action, it would have been necessary to test, and conduct research into, procedures and equipment that had been designed during the Cold War years to protect against radioactive contamination in the aftermath of nuclear war. Also, in order to be able to implement long-term protection, leaders would need to know about the immediate effects of a nuclear attack. If a multi-year plan culminating in nuclear war against the West was on the cards, could a major nuclear disaster in the Ukraine have been a useful, if tasteless, preparatory experiment?

Other theories circulating about the disaster include that it was the West's fault, for selling defective equipment to Russia as part of a wider Cold War conspiracy, or, as suggested by a home-made video posted on YouTube, that the Chernobyl explosion was caused by a US air strike.

CHRISTOPHER MARLOWE

In 1593, Christopher Marlowe, one of England's finest poets and dramatists, was stabbed to death at the age of 29 by Ingram Frizer. Historians acknowledge that his murder was probably the result of a bar brawl – a dispute over who should pay the bill, in fact – but some people believe that his violent death may well have had a political cause. Prior to his death, accusations of blasphemy, subversion and homosexuality had destroyed his public image; he was also charged with atheism on the evidence of his friend and fellow dramatist Thomas Kyd. As a result of his sacrilegious beliefs, some scholars allege that Marlowe was murdered by Sir Thomas Walsingham, a Puritan sympathizer and agent of Queen Elizabeth I. Others accuse royalists, in particular the supporters of the Earl of Essex, of his murder. Significantly, Marlowe's killer eventually received a pardon from the Queen.

In the sixteenth century, the punishments for such "crimes" as Marlowe was accused of included being boiled alive, burned at the stake, or being hanged, drawn and quartered. Taking these penalties into consideration, it is hardly surprising that some people believe that Christopher Marlowe faked his own death. Had he simply fled the country, or gone into hiding, he would have been pursued as a fugitive for the rest of his life. A much better solution would have been to stage his own demise and assume a new identity. Having allegedly worked as a spy for the government since his time at Cambridge University, Marlowe would have had both the experience and the contacts to hatch such a plan. Indeed, the fact that the coroner's inquest and subsequent burial of the body – in an unmarked grave – were completed within 48 hours of the "killing" gives even more credence to this idea.

To this day, conspiracy theories rather than facts shroud the events leading up to Marlowe's death. Though Ingram Frizer was named as the writer's killer, the real truth about Marlowe's end will probably never be known.

CORONAVIRUS

When the novel coronavirus SARS-CoV-2, which causes the disease COVID-19, was first identified, it wasn't long before conspiracy theories emerged surrounding its origins. The initial outbreak was linked to a "wet market" in Wuhan, China, in November 2019, with scientists proposing that it had made the jump there from caged live animals to humans – at first they thought that it could have come from snakes, though later scientists came to believe that bats were the original reservoir.

There were claims that the Chinese government had tried to cover up the outbreak. It was widely reported in the media that whistle-blower doctors who tried to warn about the disease were persecuted, and many also believed that China was being economical with the figures relating to the outbreak. The Chinese Communist Party certainly seemed keen to point the finger elsewhere, with a government spokesman famously tweeting in March 2020: "It might be [the] US Army who brought the epidemic to Wuhan."

As the outbreak spread across international borders and a global pandemic became increasingly likely, a more sinister theory began to circulate: a laboratory in Wuhan that was trying to devise an all-purpose vaccine created SARS-CoV-2 to give the vaccine something to work against. A dozen lab staff were said to have been infected and the unit was sealed, but one person escaped and began to spread the disease all over the city. The wet-market story was invented as a cover-up. The theory that the virus was invented as a bioweapon also became very popular, and many pointed to the fact that the Institute of Virology, which houses China's only level-four biosafety laboratory (the highest classification of labs that study deadly viruses), is situated in Wuhan.

Others were more concerned with the uncanny coincidence that the emergence of the virus coincided with the switch-on of the 5G network in China. This theory gained ground when Keri Hilson, an American singer with 4.2 million followers on Twitter, highlighted what she believed was a connection between 5G and COVID-19 in her tweets: "People have been trying to warn us about 5G for YEARS. Petitions, organizations, studies… what we're going through is the affects [sic] of radiation. 5G launched in CHINA. Nov 1, 2019. People dropped dead." Around that time, conspiracy theorists also pointed to viral videos of people "dropping on the ground and fainting" in China, which they claimed was caused by 5G radio waves messing with the oxygen levels in the victims' blood.

There was also much speculation that we had been warned about the coming of the virus, and one such warning came in the form of an episode of *The Simpsons* in 1993. A Facebook post, showing stills from the show, went viral. The stills show Homer Simpson and Principal Skinner being infected, and a news anchor reading from a piece of paper while the words "corona virus" and a cat appear on a screen behind him. It later turned out that the images were doctored. Three images were from an episode called "Osaka Flu", where a factory worker coughs into a package for Homer and he falls sick. And the text behind the news anchor actually read "Apocalypse Meow".

More eerie is the apparent warning given in the 1981 book *The Eyes of Darkness* by Dean Koontz. The plot is about a mother trying to find out what happened to her son after he mysteriously disappears on a camping trip. It turns out that the boy is being held captive in Wuhan, China, the site of a deadly virus outbreak. One passage gives details of a virus called "Wuhan-400", developed at a lab outside the city. The fictional disease's effects on the human body are similar in several respects to those of COVID-19.

Perhaps most disturbing of all were the actions of US President Donald Trump, who tweeted and uttered various myths or speculations about the disease in the early stages of the pandemic, including that the heat during the month of April would kill the virus and that the infected should consider "going to work". As Syracuse University assistant professor Whitney Phillips told *The New York Times*, "What this case will show is that conspiracy theories can kill."

DAVID KELLY

Weapons expert Dr David Kelly died in suspicious circumstances in July 2003, days after admitting to the Foreign Affairs Select Committee that he had spoken with BBC reporter Andrew Gilligan. The BBC subsequently reported that the danger Iraq posed had been exaggerated in the government dossier of September 2002, which warned the British public of the existence of certain weapons of mass destruction.

The Hutton Inquiry set out to determine whether or not the circumstances leading up to Dr Kelly's death could have had an effect on his state of mind, or whether these circumstances might have influenced the actions of others. Yet in a statement delivered by Lord Hutton on 28 January 2004, the following ruling was made: "I am satisfied that Dr Kelly took his own life by cutting his left wrist and that his death was hastened by his taking co-proxamol tablets. I am further satisfied that there was no involvement by a third person in Dr Kelly's death."

The forensic pathologist at the Hutton Inquiry, Dr Nicholas Hunt, judged that Dr Kelly bled to death from a cut to the wrist, but other experts were sceptical of this conclusion. In a letter published in *The Guardian*, medical specialists David Halpin, C. Stephen Frost and Searle Sennett expressed their view that this was "highly improbable". Dr Hunt stated that only the ulnar artery had been severed. This complete transection would cause the artery to retract and close down, enabling the blood to clot. To have died this way, Dr Kelly would have had to lose much more blood than the ambulance team had reported.

Dr Alexander Allan, the forensic toxicologist at the inquiry, said that the blood level of the drug's components was less than a third of what is normal for a fatal overdose. Halpin, Frost and Sennett concluded their letter by stating: "We dispute that Dr Kelly could have died from haemorrhage or from co-proxamol ingestion or from both." This theory raises the question of the real cause of Dr Kelly's death – and, furthermore, why it is not being made known to the public.

Dr Kelly denied that he could have been the BBC's main source and the Ministry of Defence claimed that no suggestion was made that Dr Kelly should lose his job over the issue. However, a friend of Dr Kelly, British diplomat David Broucher, told the Hutton Inquiry that in an email hours before his disappearance, Dr Kelly hinted at his crisis with lines such as "many dark actors playing games". In other conversations Dr Kelly seemed to predict his own death, saying that he would "probably be found dead in the woods" if the British invasion of Iraq was to go ahead.

In 2007, Norman Baker, Liberal Democrat MP for Lewes, published a book entitled *The Strange Death of David Kelly*; in it he presented many omissions and inconsistencies in the evidence for the case which brought the conclusion of the

Hutton Inquiry into question. He argued that Dr Kelly did not commit suicide and suggested there could have been a cover-up involving Thames Valley Police, who had been responsible for the official investigation. A member of Dr Kelly's family, however, rejected his theories, saying: "I've read it all, every word, and I don't believe it."

In 2009, Lord Hutton's findings were questioned by a group of British physicians who had not had access to the evidence. These included Dr Michael Powers QC, who was also a barrister and former coroner. Based on the published reports, they suggested that the cause of death could not have been correct, as the artery in question is small, and severing it would not have caused enough blood loss to lead to death. Several forensic pathologists, however, challenged this, saying that the combination of Dr Kelly taking an overdose and his pre-existing heart condition meant that a smaller amount of blood loss could have killed him.

In June 2010, both the *Daily Mail* and the *Mail on Sunday* claimed to have found evidence of a cover-up to hide a murder plot. A UN weapons inspector, Richard Spertzel, claimed Dr Kelly was on some sort of hit list during the last part of his life. In July of that year, a former KGB agent named Boris Karpichkov claimed he had been told Dr Kelly had been "exterminated", with his death made to look like a suicide.

In August 2010, Michael Howard, former leader of the Conservative Party, called for a full inquest. Dominic Grieve, attorney general for England and Wales, confirmed he would consider reopening the case.

The full post-mortem report was made public in October 2010, emphasising Lord Hutton's findings. It is doubtful, though, that this publication will stop theorists looking for a reason for Dr David Kelly's death, convinced it could not have been suicide.

DENVER INTERNATIONAL AIRPORT

An airport might not seem to be the obvious centre of a conspiracy, but Denver International Airport (DIA) is reported to be the secret headquarters of the Illuminati and the New World Order, making it a conspiracy hotspot. Apparently the base of operations is hidden below the airport, so as travellers go about their business they're unaware that they're walking directly over the most powerful, influential and secretive people in the world.

Others claim that, in fact, it is aliens that are housed within the airport, and others still that it is a sanctioned hideout for neo-Nazis. All claims, however, are at least partially related to the shape and overall design of the building itself. The runways make a loose swastika when looked at from above, and many of the artworks, including sculptures and engravings, are thought to be either coded messages for Illuminati, or else a secret, alien language.

Further, there is indeed an underground system below DIA. The spaces and interlinking tunnels were meant to be used as an underground baggage system and train network for the airport, but apparently the design was disastrous and this was abandoned. Theorists believe this is a cover-up, but even if the original plans were abandoned, that still leaves a whole underground network, ripe for inhabiting and developing...

For some theorists, the reason for their suspicions has humble beginnings: Denver did not need an airport when Denver International was built. Although the planners state that Denver International has a more efficient layout than the old Stapleton International, it has fewer runways, which technically reduces Denver's flight capacity. Further, the new airport was built despite widespread protest – evidence that there must have been another, more sinister reason for wanting to build the new structure.

DIANA, PRINCESS OF WALES

The sudden and brutal death of Diana, Princess of Wales in a car crash in Paris on 31 August 1997 left millions of mourners in its wake, and not a few conspiracy theories. Was it an accident, or was there a malevolent motive for her abrupt demise? It wasn't long before the fingers started to point at a host of suspects.

Speculations that Diana was deliberately killed in the culmination of a perverse master plan that had orchestrated the drunk driver and the paparazzi chase were raised the very night she died, and over the next two crucial weeks various distinct themes began to emerge. One was that she was killed by the royal family or, acting on the royals' behalf, British intelligence. Their reasoning? Was it because Prince Charles wanted to be free to marry his long-time confidante and love, Camilla Parker Bowles? Or because they did not want a Muslim, in the figure of Dodi Al Fayed, to act as stepfather to a future king of England? The BBC reported that the Libyan leader, Colonel Gaddafi, told his followers in a televised speech that the "accident" was a combined French and British conspiracy, because they did not want an Arab man to marry a British princess.

Other suggested suspects include the IRA, the CIA, Islamic militants and even the Freemasons. After all, Diana and Dodi were killed under a stonework bridge, a Masonic symbol. Or perhaps Diana was killed off by agents of international arms manufacturers to stop her crusade against landmines.

Here are several versions of the story to mull over…

MI6

If Diana was a threat to the throne, she was, many would say, a threat to the stability and well-being of the state. What better reason for elements of the secret service to wipe her out? Some members of the secret service seem to have a rather odd idea of what constitutes a threat to the state. Files exist on John Lennon and on Jack Straw, and a former secret agent claimed that MI6 once plotted to destroy the entire Labour government in the 1970s. It is not outside the realms of possibility that the same organization who believed that Lennon was capable of wreaking social and political havoc also believed that Diana was about to stir up widespread popular unrest.

What is more, MI6 were suspected of bugging Diana throughout her married life, hounding her and then releasing personal information. For example, many believe that it was they who were behind the release of "Squidgygate" that so damaged her reputation during her break-up with Charles.

Bodyguard Trevor Rees-Jones had once been a member of the Parachute Regiment and had completed two spells in Northern Ireland. He also served in the Royal Military Police. With this kind of background, it would have been almost impossible not to have come into contact with members of the secret service.

Could the fact that only he survived the crash be evidence that he was involved in the plot to kill Diana?

THE DODI TARGET

There is also the theory that Diana's death was brought about not by a plot to kill her, but rather as a result of an elaborate plan to assassinate Dodi by business enemies of his father. Certainly, the death of Diana would have been a spectacular cover-up for any such operation.

Mohamed Al Fayed has made more than a few enemies in his time. His acquisition of Harrods came about only after a bitter battle, and he was denied British nationality after questions were raised about his business negotiations and other activities. As his eldest son, Dodi would have been an obvious target for anyone wanting to address the balance with Al Fayed.

THE EGYPTIAN POINT OF VIEW

Many Egyptians were upset to find that fellow countryman Mohamed Al Fayed had been refused citizenship to Britain, and felt that the media reports placing his son's death completely in the shadow of Diana only served to contribute to the general hostility against their race. Within days of the accident, conspiracy theories had surfaced in Egypt. Columnist Anis Mansour wrote in Egypt's leading English-language newspaper, *Al-Ahram Weekly*, "British intelligence killed her to save the throne, just as the CIA killed Marilyn Monroe at the same age. When it turns to marrying a Muslim from whom she might have borne a boy named Mohamed or a girl named Fatemah and that Muslim child would be the brother of a king of England, the guardian of the church, there had to be a solution."

Some think Diana was about to announce a religious conversion. "Who killed her?" asked an account of "Diana's Conversion to Islam" in *Al-Ahram Weekly*. "British intelligence? Israeli intelligence? Or both? We believe that Diana's conversion to Islam was the reason she was killed. Hadn't she said she was going to shock the world?"

And yet some Egyptian commentators have mocked all the sensation-mongering. The *Al-Ahram Weekly* does comment on the failure of one such author to "implicate the French company that first built the tunnel into the murder."

DIANA IS ALIVE

Is Diana really dead? There's always the chance that she faked her own death, Elvis style, and that she and Dodi are now living on a deserted island somewhere far away from the paparazzi, perhaps along with Elvis, Michael Jackson and friends.

One theorist has commented how significant it was that Mother Teresa lay in state in a big, glass coffin compared to the closed casket of Diana. Dodi's casket has never even been seen, let alone open at a funeral. The official reasoning was that their faces were too badly damaged for open-casket viewing but, then, we're also told that Diana was uttering some final words.

One piece of evidence supporting this theory is that bodyguard Trevor Rees-Jones is still alive, despite claims from Mercedes experts that it would have been well nigh impossible for anyone to have survived a crash in a car going at 121 mph. Maybe, as Henri Paul's lawyers claim, the car was not going that fast. Maybe the crash was in fact faked by Rees-Jones, who had previously deposited Diana and Dodi elsewhere?

More and more bizarrely, Dodi's usual driver was not used. The mystery of Henri Paul, the security officer who only agreed to drive the vehicle at the last minute, is still unsolved. His identity was kept secret for several days after the crash. According to colleagues at the Ritz hotel, he had been something of a loner and did not socialize with them. Such little personal information seems to exist on Henri Paul that one version of the story would have it that he simply did not exist; another that he was whisked away from the hospital after being pronounced dead by doctors working with the Al Fayed family. There are also conflicting reports on how much alcohol Paul had drunk before the crash: the official report concludes that he was three times over the French legal limit, but witnesses only saw him consume two drinks, a claim unofficially verified by Lord Stevens, who oversaw the Metropolitan Police investigation of the crash.

Perhaps most suspiciously of all, Diana let slip to the *Daily Mail* just six hours before she died that she was going to withdraw completely from public life. Well, she certainly did that. Whether the crash was an impressive "death" scene from which she retreated into blissful privacy, or whether it was an attempt at a faked death that went horribly wrong, we don't know.

Plastic surgery permitting, it might be worth looking out for a stunningly attractive distant relative coming to visit Diana's children. Unless, of course, it's true what some say: that the accident was faked by aliens and she has been whisked up to the mother ship to be with Elvis.

Whatever the truth, the long-awaited inquest which started in 2004 ended in April 2008, when the jury returned a verdict of unlawful killing, attributing the accident to gross negligence by

Henri Paul, the driver, made worse by the pursuing paparazzi. Mohamed Al Fayed announced the day after the verdict that he would end his ten-year campaign to establish that it was murder, not an accident. He said he was doing it for the sake of her children.

With this campaign over it seems that, while the above theories may be held on to by some, officially the hunt for the reason for Diana's death is over.

DONALD TRUMP

Donald Trump will be remembered for many things: for his career as a real-estate mogul in New York, for hosting *The Apprentice*, for his time as President of the United States of America, for his numerous Twitter gaffes, and not least for promoting and being at the centre of some of the most controversial conspiracy theories to have circulated in our time, most notably those surrounding the presidential election of 2016.

In January 2017, American intelligence agencies – the CIA, the FBI and the NSA – jointly issued a statement with "high confidence" that the Russian government interfered in the 2016 election to favour a Trump victory. Trump was quick to reject this and to point the finger elsewhere, and has since made many claims, including that the FBI "spied" on his campaign, that Barack Obama tapped his phones, that Special Counsel Robert Mueller's Russia investigation was a "witch hunt" and that the "deep state" is out to get him.

Trump has also promoted the theory that it was Ukraine, rather than Russia, that interfered in the 2016 election

– a theory that Russia was happy to support. When the Democratic National Committee was hacked, Trump claimed that it withheld "its server" from the FBI. He also said that CrowdStrike, the company which investigated the security breach, was Ukraine-based and Ukrainian-owned and that "the server" was hidden in Ukraine. His claims have been debunked, including by some of his own advisors. (In reality there were more than 140 DNC servers and digital copies of these were given to the FBI, and CrowdStrike is based in the US – the largest owners are American companies.) The whole complicated controversy dragged on and eventually led to Trump being impeached in January 2020, though he was acquitted in February 2020.

Here are just some of the other conspiracy theories that Trump has spread in his time:

- Former president Barrack Obama was not born in the United States. In 2011 Trump claimed he deployed private investigators to discover Obama's true place of birth, and they "could not believe" what they found. When Obama released his long-form birth certificate, Trump continued to question the document's authenticity.

- The dangers of asbestos are a big "con", Trump told *New York* magazine in 1992: "There's nothing wrong except the Mob has a strong lobby in Albany because they have the dumps and control the truck."

- Trump tweeted that "3,000 people did not die in the two hurricanes that hit Puerto Rico", referring to Hurricane Maria and Irma in 2017. He claimed that Democrats inflated the death toll to make him look bad.

CONSPIRACY THEORIES

- The father of Republican presidential rival Ted Cruz, Rafael Cruz, was photographed in the early 1960s with JFK assassin Lee Harvey Oswald handing out pro-Fidel Castro leaflets.

- Vince Foster, a former aide to President Bill Clinton, who committed suicide in 1993, was in fact murdered because he had "intimate knowledge of what was going on" in the White House.

- Syrian refugees arriving in the USA were really ISIS terrorists. Trump used this as justification for his travel ban and in 2015 was recorded on Fox News saying, "They could be ISIS. It could be a plot. I mean, I don't want to think in terms of conspiracy, but it could be a plot."

- At the National Republican Congressional Committee's annual spring dinner in Washington in 2019, Trump criticized energy-producing windmills, adding that "they say the noise causes cancer".

- Former President Bill Clinton and Hilary Clinton were allegedly implicated in the death of financier and convicted sex offender Jeffrey Epstein. (See page 102 for more on Epstein's suspicious death.)

- Trump has repeatedly said that vaccines can cause autism in children. He first made this claim when speaking to a reporter from the South Florida *Sun Sentinel* in 2007: "When I was growing up, autism wasn't really a factor. And now all of a sudden, it's an epidemic... My theory is the shots. We're giving these massive injections at one time, and I really think it does something to the children."

- In 2015, in the run-up to his election campaign, Trump repeatedly spoke at rallies of how Muslims in New Jersey were filmed cheering after the 9/11 terrorist attacks on Manhattan. In a phone interview on NBC's *Meet the Press*, Trump said that hundreds of people told him they also saw televised Muslim celebrations. The footage is yet to surface, if it exists.

- Climate change is a "total, and very expensive hoax" perpetuated by the Chinese government, the aim of the hoax being to make American manufacturing non-competitive.

- During the COVID-19 pandemic, Trump claimed to have seen evidence indicating that the virus had originated in a Chinese lab. (See page 72 for more on the coronavirus pandemic and the conspiracy theories surrounding it.)

DRUGS

In *Brave New World*, Aldous Huxley depicts a totalitarian regime where the government maintains their power by inflicting drugs on their citizens. The novel is set in a dystopian future, but the reality that it depicts may not be so far from the truth.

Andrew Cooper, the publisher of the Brooklyn weekly newspaper *The City Sun*, put forward the theory that white middle-class communities push heroin into the black communities to divert the young from political activity.

Rumours that the US government are dumping drugs in black neighbourhoods go back at least as far as the Vietnam War years, when heroin was allegedly promoted to stop the increasing militancy within the black community across the nation. Political black activist Dick Gregory said that: "Nothing in the history of the planet is as vile as what we're about to uncover. As bad as slavery was, white folks never accused us of jumping on the boat." But, he continued, black people have been blamed for the uprising of drugs.

DRUGS

And it would seem that this situation is not unique to the African American communities. Senator John Kerry of Massachusetts carried out an investigation into what he saw as the drug conspiracy, concluding that the CIA and the US government knew about and participated in cocaine smuggling in cahoots with Nicaraguan drug barons, as part of an elaborate ploy to overthrow the former left-wing government of Nicaragua.

EBOLA

Conspiracy theories about outbreaks of Ebola in the Democratic Republic of Congo (originally called Zaire, after which the main strain of the virus, Ebola-Zaire, is named) run as rife as the disease itself. Ebola is a virus that incubates inside its human hosts in under two weeks, turning internal organs to pulp and causing severe blood clots, haemorrhaging and brain damage. Moreover, potential drugs and vaccines are still being developed and tested for the successful treatment of Ebola.

Almost 300 people died in the original outbreak in 1976, and dozens of cases have been documented since within the Democratic Republic of Congo, including an outbreak in 2007 which killed 187 people. A new strain of Ebola was discovered in Uganda in 2007, infecting nearly 150 people. In 2014, there was another outbreak, this time primarily affecting Liberia, Sierra Leone and Guinea. So far the virus has killed thousands of people in Africa alone. The 2014 outbreak spread to the West, although it was controlled, with one death in the US. There have been further outbreaks in the region since.

EBOLA

Ebola theories parallel suspicions that AIDS is a man-made killer designed to eliminate the world's so-called "useless eaters": black people, homosexuals and drug users. Could outbreaks of Ebola have been engineered? Could the US military, or the New World Order, or the United Nations, or the Center for Disease Control and Prevention have developed a lethal virus to expunge those aforementioned useless eaters? Or even to develop a worldwide epidemic? Whatever the truth, the idea of such a disease being purposefully designed and executed is truly sinister.

ECHELON

Those living in the Western world became accustomed to increasing openness and democracy in their governments throughout the last decades of the twentieth century and the beginning of the twenty-first, but in one area there remains profound secrecy and confidentiality: the role of spies. Governments' reticence to discuss matters, both significant and trivial, relating to security services has created suspicion of illicit or clandestine operations carried out in our name.

At the heart of people's fears is the question of just who MI5 and MI6 may be spying upon. Next time you make a phone call, send an email or fax, be careful what you say and write because someone could be eavesdropping. Despite the implementation of privacy and human rights laws in many countries, rumours have continued for several years that there is an enormous electronic surveillance machine intercepting all international communications traffic across the world and processing it through giant supercomputers. These rumours have persisted since the beginning of the Cold War but, in the 1980s, formal proof of this Orwellian scheme emerged. Intelligence chiefs in

New Zealand felt impelled by their consciences to admit what had been going on for a generation. A system called Echelon had been developed following a treaty known as the UK–US Security Agreement, signed in 1947 between the governments of the US, the UK, Canada, Australia and New Zealand.

This alliance aimed to create a global intelligence network with a vast pool of information for analysis by the security services of the treaty's signatories. Although it is illegal for the UK and US security services to spy on their respective citizens and companies, the members of the alliance managed to neatly sidestep national laws by spying on each other. So, for example, if MI6 wanted to spy on a suspect individual in London, rather than go through the lengthy process of applying for a warrant, they could simply get their US counterparts to do it for them and then share the information.

The system was designed by the US National Security Agency, who have access to all of the information; the other members may only view the specific sectors of the collected intelligence relevant to their particular spheres of influence. The centrepiece of the whole operation is the Echelon dictionary, a vast resource of keywords, including names, subjects, locations, telephone numbers and email addresses. The millions of daily communications around the world are automatically scanned to pick up recognized words, phrases, numbers and addresses. Every match is then transcribed and used by intelligence gatherers.

The system has already provoked the ire of European Union countries that aren't members of the pact. The issue was so sensitive that a European Parliament report was commissioned to look into the affair. "It is a very dangerous attack on the sovereignty of member states," complained one MEP (Member of the European Parliament). The French government were angered by what they believe is illegal tapping of government and business communications, with information shared solely among Echelon allies. The European report cited "wide-ranging evidence" that information is used "to provide commercial advantages to companies". The French press has made claims that Boeing was provided with secret information to deprive Airbus, its European rival, of contracts.

Clearly, this system has significant uses in combating terrorism, crime and threats to national security, but its implications for civil liberties and its dubious legal authority raise vital questions for citizens and politicians alike. The lack of formal acknowledgement of its existence, or its precise composition and function, inspire those with conspiratorial minds to question just what, precisely, is going on.

THE ELECTRONIC BANKING CONSPIRACY

This theory is intrinsically linked to the Illuminati and the New World Order, and the theories surrounding the secretive super-organization whose sole aim is to control the world, ensuring that whatever happens benefits its members.

The theory is that electronic banking is to be used as a means of controlling the masses, and that the preparations and early phases of this plan have been happening since antiquity. This is a theory which has been explored in fiction, with Margaret Atwood touching on the subject in *The Handmaid's Tale*, and with recent sci-fi series *Revolution* focusing on it as its central theme.

The first phase of the theory was the replacement of currency based on precious metals in coin form with paper notes, a process which began during the Renaissance. Next came the appearance of virtual money – credit cards – where tangible objects were replaced with numerical data encoded on a magnetic strip. In step three, e-commerce boomed, with many websites not even requiring credit cards to buy and sell over the internet. Phase four is the concentration of worldwide banking into the hands of the few, with large international conglomerate banks making it easier for finances to be controlled. Next, the worldwide implementation of an electronic identity card. The final stage, which it would seem we are now close to, is that a huge disaster will be engineered, causing a worldwide blackout, destroying all data and therefore all electronic accounts. As the population will be left with nothing, the New World Order will be able to rise up and control the now poverty-struck and chaotic world.

Theorists have it that the blackout will be preceded by test blackouts on a smaller scale; indeed, shortly after 9/11, blackouts occurred almost simultaneously in the US, the UK, Canada and Australia.

Perhaps it's time to stop relying on virtual money – or is it already too late?

ELVIS PRESLEY

If Elvis Presley was an agent for the CIA, then most people are unaware of this fact – and are blind to the implications. As certain theorists explain, Elvis' rise in popularity would have provided the perfect cover for a top-secret military installation in the heart of Memphis, Tennessee. The fact that the site was so high profile would have meant that CIA officials could be as open as they wanted, for surely no one, internal or foreign, would ever suspect an international celebrity's home as a headquarters for an international spy network. Obviously some precautions would have been necessary. Theorists maintain that in order to prevent a suspicious number of government vehicles congregating in Elvis' driveway, an extensive system of tunnels was created, some extending for several hundred metres. At Agent Presley's death, the government took precautionary measures to ensure that the mansion remained within the Presley family. Rumour has it that, despite the constant waves of tourists to Graceland, the tunnel network is in continuous use.

Quite apart from his alleged underhand dealings with the CIA, there seems to be another side to Elvis that is little known.

CONSPIRACY THEORIES

The suggestion that Elvis may have killed charismatic President John F. Kennedy for having hogged the media coverage is not to be missed. If Elvis did indeed kill Kennedy, the question remains as to who killed Elvis. And if jealousy over media coverage was one reason for Kennedy's assassination, it would make sense that John Lennon was overcome by a similar pique of jealousy and killed Elvis to make way for his own publicity.

And the conspiracy doesn't end there. It would appear that Lennon didn't consider Elvis' influence. The theory alleges that the tragic assassination of the former Beatle in 1980 might have been carried out by Elvis supporter Michael Jackson, who, in turn, closed the circle of conspiracy and gave the whole thing away by marrying Elvis' daughter, Lisa Marie Presley. Jackson's own fate, it would seem, could have been meted out by one of Lennon's fans – or perhaps even a member of the Beatles. The celebrity world is nothing if not incestuous.

But probably the best-known conspiracy theory surrounding Elvis has it that he didn't die on 16 August 1977 but is actually still alive. There is a huge number of reasons given for suspecting that Elvis faked his own death, some more convincing than others. Several funeral guests reported that there were discrepancies between the body in the coffin and Elvis' appearance in life, including a differently shaped nose and eyebrows, and soft hands rather than the calloused hands caused by his martial arts practice. Some say that the body was not Elvis but a wax replica designed to pull the wool over the eyes of the funeral-goers. On top of that, a former lover received a rose the day after his death, with a card signed *El Lancelot*, her pet name for Elvis which she claimed no one else knew.

Motives for his faked death are also surprisingly easy to find. Just before his "death", Elvis lost around $10,000,000 in a property deal connected to the Mafia, and there's speculation that the government offered him a new identity and safe relocation in return for testifying against the organized crime ring. He was also reported to have been extremely conscious of his burgeoning weight and increasingly poor performances, so "dying" may have seemed the easiest way out of a faltering show-business career. Elvis had already faked his death once before, when he arranged for someone to "shoot" him (the gun contained blanks and he had a mechanism for releasing fake blood), so he knew how to do it.

Sightings of Elvis continue to be reported around the world, including a mysterious masked singer who appears under the name of Orion, and who looks and sounds like Elvis, as well as the ubiquitous claims that he is working in a burger bar. The truth is that if Elvis really did fake his own death, we're very unlikely to find out.

EPSTEIN DIDN'T KILL HIMSELF

Jeffrey Edward Epstein was an American financier who procured many women, including underage girls, who were then sexually abused by Epstein and some of his contacts from elite social circles. In 2008 Epstein pleaded guilty and was convicted by a Florida state court of soliciting a prostitute and of procuring an underage girl for prostitution. He served almost 13 months in custody. He was arrested again in July 2019 on federal charges for the sex trafficking of dozens of minors in Florida and New York, some as young as 14.

On the morning of 10 August, Epstein was found unresponsive in his cell in New York City, where he was imprisoned awaiting trial. He was taken to a local hospital to be treated for life-threatening injuries and was subsequently pronounced dead by the hospital staff. New York City's chief medical examiner, Barbara Sampson, ruled his death a suicide by hanging.

Epstein's lawyers were quick to challenge that conclusion and launched their own investigation. Michael Baden was hired to oversee the autopsy and he suggested that the autopsy evidence was more indicative of homicidal strangulation. Epstein had links with many powerful men, including presidents Trump and Clinton, and he had claimed to have compromising information about various influential people. This, coupled with reports of violations of normal jail procedures on the night of his death, led to much speculation that he was in fact murdered.

The phrase "Epstein didn't kill himself" became a meme that went viral overnight on social media. Its rise to prominence was helped along when a Fox News segment showing a former Navy SEAL being interviewed about military dogs ended with the SEAL blurting out the phrase. It circulated on popular social media platform TikTok and was graffitied onto the side of buildings. Arizona Republican Congressman Paul Gosar shared a series of 23 tweets, the first letter of each of which spelled out the phrase. When Australian rapper Matthew Lambert won the 2019 ARIA Music Award for Best Australian Live Act, he included the phrase in his acceptance speech. And two beer companies, Rusted Spoke Brewing Co. and Tactical OPS Brewing, advertised special-edition beers in connection with the meme.

THE EVERLASTING LIGHT BULB

Just imagine never having to replace a light bulb again. Of course, with modern energy-saving bulbs, replacement is needed far less frequently, but they do still have a finite lifespan. Well, the everlasting light bulb could do away with all that, and theorists have it that this item was created many years ago, but that it has been suppressed in order to make us, the public, continue to buy disposable products.

This idea was given some weight by the existence of the Phoebus Cartel, which included OSRAM, Philips and General Electric – and which controlled the manufacture and sale of light bulbs. The cartel has featured in popular culture, blurring the lines between fact and fiction.

A somewhat softer version of this theory argues that light bulbs have a planned lifespan which is far shorter than their actual capability, known as "planned obsolescence". This means that companies continue to make large profits by forcing consumers to buy more of a product which is, essentially, built to fail.

FINLAND DOESN'T EXIST

It all started on Reddit when one user replied to a thread about the scariest things your parents ever told you, saying that he learned from his parents that Finland does not exist. What began as a joke quickly gained traction online, spawning numerous subreddits and posts explaining how the world came to believe in a country that simply isn't there.

So if Finland doesn't exist, how did people come to believe in its existence, and what's really there on the map where it's supposed to be? Finland-deniers allege that world maps have been altered as part of a UN conspiracy to keep people believing in Finland. The idea that an entire country is made up is so bizarre that nobody would ever believe it – which is why it was so easy to do. And what about all those pesky "Finns"? According to the conspiracy theorists, these people, who genuinely believe they are from and live in Finland, are actually from small towns in eastern Sweden, western Russia and northern Estonia. Helsinki, Finland's largest city and capital, exists in eastern Sweden.

But why would anyone want to invent a country? Well, a lot of it could be to do with Japanese fishing rights. It's well known that the Japanese love sushi, but they had overfished in Japanese waters and because of tight fishing regulations they weren't able to fish as much as they wanted to meet demand. After the Cold War (or World War Two, according to some accounts) they agreed with Russia to tweak maps to indicate that there was a "landmass" where there was not one in reality – the area covered by the landmass on maps was actually an area of the Baltic Sea, where the Japanese could fish, and they have been doing so ever since. The fish caught there was transported through Russia on the Trans-Siberian railway and a small percentage of it was given to the local population (who were starving at the time), and then it was shipped on to Japan. This is believed to be still happening today, and the packets of fish now arrive in Japan disguised as Nokia products.

FLAT EARTH

"Flat Earthers" are people who believe that the Earth is flat. According to them, the truth about our planet's shape is being covered up in a "round Earth conspiracy" coordinated by NASA and other shady government agencies. Flat Earthers hold that the Earth looks flat when you walk around on it, so therefore it must be flat. For them, seeing is believing.

Our predecessors in the far-off ancient past were also of the Flat Earth persuasion. The Ancient Greeks were the first to have an inkling of Earth's roundness: around 350 BCE Aristotle wrote in his treatise *On the Heavens* that the Earth is circular, and Eratosthenes (*c.*276–194 BCE) managed to measure the Earth's circumference. Much later, in 1519–22, an expedition initiated by Portuguese explorer Ferdinand Magellan and completed by Juan Sebastián Elcano circumnavigated the Earth, which would have been a bit tricky if it had an edge. Since then, most people have been convinced that the Earth is a globe.

The idea of a flat Earth resurfaced in the late nineteenth century when English writer Samuel Rowbotham (1816–84) published a pamphlet called *Zetetic Astronomy*, in which he posited that the Earth is a plane or disc with the North Pole at its centre, bounded along its perimeter by a wall of ice, and that the sun, moon, planets and stars move only several hundred miles above the Earth's surface. After he died, Lady Elizabeth Blount established a Universal Zetetic Society, named after Rowbotham's version of astronomy, whose objective was to propagate his ideas. This was succeeded in 1956 by Samuel Shenton's International Flat Earth Research Society. In 1971, Shenton died and Charles K. Johnson inherited part of Shenton's library. He became president of the International Flat Earth Research Society of America and over the next three decades membership is reported to have reached 3,500. A fire destroyed most of its records in 1997 and it went into decline, but was revived in 2004, eventually leading to the official relaunch of the society in October 2009.

The society has been growing in membership steadily ever since, and there are many other groups and individuals who are part of the Flat Earth movement. There is an annual Flat Earth International Conference in the US and other conventions have been held in Brazil, Britain and Italy. In 2018 a Netflix documentary called *Behind the Curve* was released, bringing the theories to a mainstream audience. Several celebrities have pledged their support for the theory, including NBA players Shaquille O'Neal and Kyrie Irving, and rapper-singer Bobby Ray Simmons Jr (known as B.o.B), who got into a Twitter battle on the matter with astrophysicist Neil deGrasse Tyson.

So what do these modern-day Flat Earthers make of all those satellite photos that show the Earth as a globe? They propose that the images are fakes, photoshopped by NASA. And while pilots may *think* they are flying in across the world, that's only because all aeroplane GPS devices have been rigged – in reality, the planes are whizzing around in circles above our disc-shaped home.

Why would NASA go to such lengths to keep Earth's true form a secret? The Flat Earth Society suggests their motivation is financial: the cost of faking a space programme would be much lower than actually having one, and those in on the conspiracy benefit from the funding the government puts into NASA and other space agencies.

If the world's scientific community have got it wrong about the Earth being a sphere, they may well have got a whole lot of other things wrong, too. In light of this, Flat Earthers have reassessed a lot of what is taught in school and come up with the following alternative theories:

- A Flat Earth geographer would inform you that the Earth is a disc with the Arctic Circle in its centre, while Antarctica, a 150-foot-tall wall of ice, sits around the rim. What's to stop people falling off? NASA employees guard the ice wall to prevent people from climbing up and falling over the edge.

- The Flat Earther take on astronomy explains that day and night are not caused by the Earth rotating on its axis as it orbits the sun. The sun, unlike the Earth, *is* a sphere 32 miles (51 km) in diameter that moves in circles 3,000 miles (4,828 km) above the plane of the Earth. It illuminates the different time zone sections of the planet in a 24-hour cycle. The moon is also a sphere, the same size as the sun, and lunar eclipses happen when an invisible "anti-moon" obscures the moon. Stars are also spheres, moving in a plane thousands of miles above the surface of the Earth.

CONSPIRACY THEORIES

- When it comes to physics, Flat Earthers have suggested that Earth's gravity is an illusion. When objects fall, they do not accelerate downward; the Earth disc accelerates upward at 32 feet per second squared (9.8 metres per second squared), driven by a force enigmatically named "dark energy".

FLIGHT AF447

On the evening of 31 May 2009, Air France flight 447 took off from Rio de Janeiro-Galeão International Airport bound for Paris, France. It never arrived. A crew of 12 and 216 passengers were lost, including 72 French citizens and 59 Brazilians.

All contact with the plane ended as it approached the outer limits of Brazilian radar surveillance, over the Atlantic Ocean. The authorities blamed bad weather, in particular multiple thunderstorms, and a subsequent catastrophic systems failure, but more sinister theories exist as to its disappearance.

One theory goes that the US government was behind the downing of Air France flight 447. The plane was allegedly zapped from the sky by a new airborne laser being tested by military officials from the US keen to demonstrate the potency of their latest invention to a sceptical Obama administration. The effectiveness of the weapon could explain why it took days of searching to find any trace of wreckage and bodies, and why the black boxes were not located until two years later.

Some theorists even suggest that the passengers never boarded the stricken flight because it was due to be used as target practice. Instead, all those booked on to the flight were whisked off to the Colorado coal mines by the US government to help boost production at a time of severe domestic economic recession. Was the delay in locating the supposed wreckage a safeguard against any early problems with the plan?

Or was Air France flight 447 hijacked by a new breed of African pirates, driven from the West African waters by rising competition and increasingly hostile foreign military interventions? The pilots could have been made to fly the plane low to evade radar detection and forced to land somewhere along the lawless West African coast. The plane was heading into Senegalese-controlled airspace when it vanished.

There have even been claims that the plane's disappearance was the work of a temporary alliance between the region's drug cartels and shadowy government figures, their goal being to dispose of passenger Pablo Dreyfus, an Argentine arms controller whose vociferous pursuit of greater controls over the illegal arms and drugs trade was making life difficult for South America's drug traffickers and unscrupulous politicians.

In May 2011 the aircraft's flight recorders were discovered and a subsequent report by France's Bureau d'Enquêtes et d'Analyses pour la Sécurité de l'Aviation Civile (BEA) published in July 2012 determined that the aircraft crashed after temporary inconsistencies between the airspeed measurements caused the autopilot to disconnect, ultimately putting the aircraft into an aerodynamic stall.

FLIGHT MH370

Malaysia Airlines flight MH370 disappeared on 8 March 2014. Extensive searches were carried out, and during 2015 and 2016 several pieces of marine debris confirmed to be from the aircraft washed ashore in the western Indian Ocean. And yet nobody has been able to determine what happened to the plane. This strange occurrence has led to a large number of different theories being put forward.

One theory suggests that the flight was shot down accidentally, as part of a military exercise in the South China Sea, and that this fact was subsequently covered up. This was explored in the book *Flight MH370: The Mystery* by Nigel Cawthorne, but, of course, nobody has found conclusive evidence of either the exercise or the shooting.

Another theory suggests that the plane was hijacked in a 9/11-style attack. This theory tells us that the plane, far from having crashed, is being hidden – that it's in the hands of terrorists who could be retrofitting the vehicle with all manner of weapons, preparing for an attack which could, according to one YouTube video, "literally destroy and blow up an entire American city".

Yet another theory, which has been staunchly denied by officials, is that the plane was redirected and landed on Diego Garcia, a British overseas territory in the Indian Ocean which also happens to be the location of a large US military base. This theory has been particularly popular in China, home to many of the passengers who disappeared along with the flight. Theorists believe that the CIA wanted something or someone aboard the flight, so they forced it to land, dismantled it in a hangar on the island, then burned the evidence and dumped it in the sea. As with the other theories, no solid evidence of this has been found.

A more basic, yet still disturbing, suggestion is that the disappearance was a deliberate act by somebody on board the plane – an act of terrorism or revenge. The fact that the plane caused no traceable damage and that most of the wreckage hasn't been found could suggest that the target was either a passenger or Malaysia Airlines, with the possible aim of discrediting the airline and making it appear unsafe.

Two outlandish theories have just as much evidence supporting them as any of the others already mentioned. Firstly, there is the theory that the plane disappeared because it was the subject of an attack using a new, sophisticated weapon, the existence of which is being covered up. Mike Adams, a well-known theorist who runs the website Natural News, suggested such a weapon was capable of removing "airplanes out of the sky without leaving behind even a shred of evidence".

And finally, one of the most popular theories despite its complexity, is the "plane switch". This suggests that Flight MH17, the Malaysia Airlines plane shot down in the Ukraine in July 2014, was in fact Flight MH370, and that the whole thing was a ruse to dispose of the plane and people. It isn't clear whether Flight MH17 existed and was physically switched – in which case, another plane is still missing – or whether the second flight was actually Flight MH370 from the start.

Perhaps it's the lack of evidence that makes this case so chilling, but until something is found, none of these theories can be proved one way or the other.

FLUORIDE

We'd all like strong bones and teeth, but at what cost? The addition of fluoride to drinking systems in Western countries has long been a source of controversy. Could it be quietly wreaking havoc on our species? There is concern that information is being withheld from the public in a massive cover-up.

In high enough doses, fluoride is fatal. While lethal levels have never been recorded in drinking water, some think a communist plot is in place to increase these levels and cause mass disruption in the West.

Others point to the alleged involvement of the aluminium industry in the increased use of fluoride in water, saying that it has a vested interest in expanding fluoridation – fluoride is a waste product of the aluminium manufacturing process and the most cost-effective way to get rid of it is to put it into the water system.

There is no denying that fluoride does initially strengthen bones and teeth, but the benefits are short-lived and there comes a point when genetic damage occurs. Bones can be weakened by fluoride to the point of complete dissolution. Theorists predict that, within seven generations, offspring of fluoridated populations could be born without any skeleton at all.

This theory provokes the serious concern that there's a dreadful fate in store for the entire Western world. Furthermore, the question is raised as to whether the potentially dire consequences were known when fluoride was introduced into our water supply. Could this be yet another disturbing attempt to curb population growth?

FOOD ADDITIVES

Just as sugar has come under fire from conspiracy theorists, so too have food additives. Any food which has undergone processing will contain some additives, be they preservatives, flavourings, sweeteners or improvers. Some of these are natural compounds, others artificial – and it is this second group which is most vilified. Of course, it is well known that eating natural foods is the healthiest course of action, but when even fruit bought from a supermarket is unnaturally glazed, it can be hard to do this.

Theorists claim that additives are proliferating to keep consumers consuming – they are designed to be addictive, and to keep people coming back to the same unhealthy foods time and again, fuelled by cravings. One additive in particular which falls into this camp is MSG (Monosodium glutamate), which is found naturally in some foods, such as mushrooms, and which creates a moreish, savoury flavour. Added to low-quality foods in its refined, white powder form, MSG gives the impression of something delicious, and leaves people wanting to go back for more. Many claim the substance itself is essentially an addictive drug.

FOOD ADDITIVES

Another additive which is heavily criticized, and which the scientific community seems to be divided on, is aspartame. This artificial sweetener is heavily used in soft drinks, particularly diet drinks – which are sold as "healthy" products and therefore widely consumed. Aspartame may taste sweet, but according to many it's a carcinogen (a substance that can cause cancer), it affects brain function and can essentially pickle us from the inside if used over a long period of time. As with many other additives, it is seen as addictive, with people not enjoying the taste of sugared soft drinks after drinking low-calorie, aspartame-sweetened diet sodas.

Whether the theorists are right or not, the only way to avoid these substances is to eat a natural, balanced diet, and not wanting to end up an addict is as good a reason as any to start.

FREEMASONRY

Dating from the sixteenth century, Freemasonry is a well-known, worldwide fraternity. Comprising an estimated five million members, it is dedicated to charitable work and the promotion of moral correctness, and believes in the existence of a supreme being. However, some think that this secret society has a much more subversive agenda.

One theory exists that the Freemasons are a cover for the Illuminati, a powerful group of prominent figures that exert covert control over many important aspects of government and society. It is speculated that the goal of the Illuminati is to create a New World Order in which the world will be ruled as a fascist state by a single government.

According to another theory, within the walls of the Masonic lodges, it is not a New World Order conspiracy at work, but a Jewish one. This theory states that the Grand Masters and lodge officers are prominent Jewish politicians, businessmen and other figures that use the fraternal network to advance their ambitions of world domination. Hitler's persecution of Freemasons during World War Two, with thousands interned and executed as political prisoners, suggests that he believed in the role of Judaism in the sect.

Others believe that the Freemasons are a devil-worshipping cult whose main purpose is to usher in the rule of Satan and bring Christianity to its knees. The Freemasons' worship of a supreme being is considered by these theorists as evidence of the organization's occult nature and its desire to see Lucifer installed as the world's commander-in-chief.

According to those who see them as manipulators of global events over the last five centuries, the Freemasons are the invisible hand behind a wide range of major events. Were the Freemasons responsible for the assassination of JFK, a US president who wouldn't bow to their influence? Does the resemblance of the Jack the Ripper murders to the Masonic initiation rituals of the time point toward the true identity of London's most notorious serial killer? Did the Freemasons fake the Apollo moon landings? Was the 9/11 attack on New York part of a religious war between Freemasonry and Islam?

FUKUSHIMA DAIICHI NUCLEAR DISASTER

The Fukushima Daiichi nuclear disaster began on 11 March 2011. It happened when the nuclear plant was hit by a tsunami caused by an earthquake, and resulted in three of the plant's six nuclear reactors going into meltdown. From 12 March onward, substantial amounts of nuclear material were released into the surrounding area and made this the largest nuclear disaster since Chernobyl, measuring level seven, the highest level, on the International Nuclear Event Scale (INES). There has since been a significant amount of radioactive water in the area, something which has proved difficult to remedy.

The commission which looked into the disaster found that it was, in effect, man-made, as its direct causes were foreseeable and those in charge failed to meet even the most basic of safety requirements. The plant was incapable of withstanding the earthquake and tsunami, something which is unacceptable, particularly in such an earthquake-prone part of the world. While this in and of itself is shocking, theorists believe the conspiracy runs deeper, and that the truth of what happened – the full extent – is being systematically hidden from us.

Some theorists are particularly concerned about radioactive water from Fukushima entering the Pacific Ocean, which could build up within the food chain. Despite containment efforts, contaminated water is still entering the Pacific each and every day. It's feared that this will cause long-term issues, such as higher cancer rates. Furthermore, although it has been several years since the original disaster, current estimates show that it could take decades to finish the necessary clean-up.

Additionally, there are hundreds of nuclear rods that need to be removed from Fukushima, and theorists are concerned that many people don't seem to be aware of the dangers involved. Computer-guided removal is impossible due to the damage the plant sustained, and manual removal poses much greater risks. Also, according to Reuters, the combined amount of caesium-137 in the aforementioned rods is thousands of times greater than the amount released when the US bombed Hiroshima. Theorists believe that the danger is extremely severe, and that the issues with the health of fish along the west coast of Canada demonstrate how geographically wide-reaching the fallout from the disaster may yet be; the affected fish bled from their gills, bellies and eyes.

Aside from the water-related issues, dozens of former sailors and marines claim they have radiation sickness as a direct result of serving aboard US Navy ships stationed near Fukushima. They're so convinced of the cause of their illness that they're suing for damages.

Whether the truth is being covered up or not, the fact that officials could be so lax as to let this disaster happen in the first place is enough to instil fear in the hearts of just about everyone. These are dangerous times we live in.

GEORGE W. BUSH AND WMDs

The American invasion of Iraq is probably etched on the memory of everyone who was alive and old enough at the time to witness its events. However, many believe that George W. Bush lied about the weapons of mass destruction (WMDs) that were the official reason for the invasion; in fact, 44 per cent of Americans believe this to be the case.

The theory is this: Bush wanted revenge. After the Gulf War, Saddam Hussein wasn't removed from power, partly due to George Bush Sr's fears that this would further unsettle the Middle East. This did not lead to better relations between Iraq and the US, with Hussein reportedly sending death threats to Bush Sr.

So it's thought that George W. Bush wanted to make Hussein pay for threatening his father – perhaps trying at the same time to prove himself. He needed a reason to send troops, and "reports" of chemical WMDs was certainly a good reason on paper. Of course, it is possible that the claim that the WMDs were simply sent to Syria to avoid being found by the US is correct. However, it is also true that no such weapons were ever found, and that direct orders were given that the first US soldier to encounter Hussein should tell him, in Arabic, "Regards from President Bush."

GLOBAL ECONOMIC RECESSION

As the effects took hold from December 2007, the fledgling twenty-first century witnessed a spectacular global economic recession. Many large industrialized countries endured the worst downturn in generations. This misery also washed up on the shores of the developing world. But who or what caused it?

It is claimed that capitalism was moments away from catastrophic collapse. The banking sector was rocked to its core, international trade was decimated, commodity prices fell through the floor and unemployment soared. The US was found with the smoking gun – mortgage lending of staggering incompetence – but who pulled the trigger?

According to one theory, a shadowy cabal – comprising some of the wealthiest people on earth, top politicians, the corporate elite and members of the most powerful aristocracies – was responsible for the financial meltdown, which was orchestrated as part of a plan to take control of the world.

The supposed activity of this New World Order, whose goal is to create a fascist One World Government, is documented through the ages and is claimed to be behind major wars, pandemics and natural disasters. Its influence is believed to have infiltrated every corridor of power and it is said that the group was able to engineer the recession using the Federal Reserve Bank in the US.

Were the banks that went bankrupt, or were only saved by huge public financial assistance, the lenders that had resisted the influence of this group? Was the recession a device to shift more power to the politicians, captains of industry and oligarchs who are members of this secret clan?

Others believe that the US government caused the fiscal turmoil in order to reduce illegal immigration. What should be made of the fact that, from the end of 2007, the number of people unlawfully entering the US fell dramatically? And isn't it true that the vast majority of consumers left homeless and penniless by the burst of the property bubble were of Hispanic and black ethnicity, two groups into which a lot of illegal immigrants fall?

Another theory points the finger of blame at a secret alliance of industrialized governments, which ushered in a period of severe global austerity as a means of crushing the financing of terrorism. By choking fiscal supply routes to increasingly well-funded and organized cells, this group hoped to neuter the likes of al-Qaeda and other militant factions that have been behind bombings and various attacks across the world.

GLOBAL WARMING

Global warming: a twentieth-century event that has become a twenty-first-century anxiety. Thanks to an increase in greenhouse gases emitted as a result of humankind's environmental negligence and consumption of fossil fuels, our planet is becoming dangerously overheated. The world worries. But is it merely one of history's greatest ever hoaxes? Some would say it is.

Many global-warming sceptics suggest that there is no reliable evidence to indicate that the globe is getting hotter by any substantial degree; they assert that what the world is witnessing is just a natural fluctuation in temperature. These people claim that, behind the science and ecological campaigning, there lie sinister motivations.

According to one theory, propagation of the "global warming" agenda is all part of a UN-sponsored plan to redistribute wealth by stunting industrial development in the West, and in particular in the US, in favour of the expansion of major emerging world markets, such as China, Brazil and India. These theorists claim that the actions of the United

Nations with regard to climate change are merely a cover created to help facilitate this shift in global finances and that the Kyoto Protocol and the Paris Agreement represent a thinly veiled attack on the US and its power base.

Others place an Illuminati-like New World Order behind global-warming fakery. Why would this group create such a fear-inducing illusion? It is believed that they have done so in order to destabilize the US economy and make it vulnerable to an attack that forms part of an alleged plot to create a fascist One World Government.

If the US was to comply with the emissions limits included in the Kyoto Protocol and Paris Agreement, would its industry not face a massive restructuring bill and job losses on a crippling scale? Wouldn't the investment required from the government mean millions of dollars siphoned away from defence, weakening the country against a possible military threat?

Others claim that global warming is a convenient truth expounded by environmentalists and scientists in order to generate more funding, a ploy in which the media colludes to guarantee the news that ensures continued sales and advertising revenues. It is even said that some governments are willing co-conspirators as the subject gives them a popular vehicle on which they can pursue other agendas.

Another take on global warming is that it is a government-created lie intended to raise more taxes from companies and individuals. Why do the voices of environmental concern shout the loudest at a time when many of the world's governments find their countries virtually broke and with precious few resources for rebuilding?

Of course, the conspiracy theory is a two-way street. Some theorists suggest that US energy companies created the "global warming is a hoax" conspiracy in order to prevent the introduction of regulatory reform, which would damage their profit margins. They claim that it is fearful elites in the oil and coal industries, who have the most to lose if the US were to cooperate with the Kyoto Protocol and Paris Agreement, that are behind the high-profile dissent.

GRETA THUNBERG ISN'T WHO SHE SAYS SHE IS

Since she stepped onto the global stage as a key instigator of the school climate-strike movement, Swedish teenager Greta Thunberg has received recognition for her efforts to convince world leaders of the need for urgent action on the climate crisis. She was, for example, named *Time* Person of the Year in 2019. But she has also been the target of a fair amount of flak from those unsympathetic to her cause. Leaving aside the personal attacks by certain political and oil industry leaders, and by climate-change-denying internet trolls, she has also been the subject of a couple of pretty out-there conspiracy theories.

One is the belief that she is actually Estella Renee, an Australian deep-state crisis actor (a performer hired by a shady body of people believed to be involved in the manipulation of government policy). One outspoken internet pundit described her as a "talented Shakespearian actress" who can do Scandinavian accents and cry at will.

Many have pushed back by pointing out that Greta's background is well documented: she has been nominated for numerous awards, has met with several world leaders, took a highly publicized voyage across the Atlantic Ocean, and the identities of her parents, Svante Thunberg and Malena Ernman, as well as her grandfather, Olof Thunberg, and her sister, Beata, are all known.

Perhaps more bizarre than the accusation that Greta is a crisis actor is the claim that she's a time traveller. Proponents of this theory point to a photo depicting a girl who bears an uncanny resemblance to Greta. The photo, believed to have been taken around 1898 and found in archives at the University of Washington, shows three children working at a gold mine in Canada. One of them is a girl with Thunberg's braided hairdo and stern expression. When the photo was circulated on Twitter in 2019, it drew a lot of attention, with one user proclaiming that if Greta Thunberg really is a time traveller, "we have to listen" to her.

THE GULF WAR COVER-UP

During the Gulf War in the late twentieth century, the world was astounded at the superiority of the US war effort. Iraqi armies were overtaken by a ratio of about 1,000:1, and the US troops returned alive.

But that is not to say that they came back healthy; thousands of war veterans have died or are dying from what has commonly come to be known as Gulf War syndrome. Symptoms are wide-ranging and include headaches, dizziness and loss of balance, memory problems, chronic fatigue, loss of muscle control, muscle and joint pain, indigestion, skin problems, shortness of breath and even insulin resistance. Scientists' attempts to locate the precise origins of Gulf War syndrome are not helped by the government's staunch denial that such a thing exists.

It is thought that it could have been caused by some sort of biological warfare agent. Whoever created this weapon allegedly used the HIV gene – the illness targets those with weak immune systems. But no one seems to know what the real story is. Lack of funding as well as pressure from the government to cover up what has really gone on has hampered extensive research. It would seem that the M. D. Anderson Cancer Center in Houston, Texas, is the only place where this syndrome is being taken seriously.

The government has released documents containing evidence to suggest that Gulf War veterans are indeed right when they claim that they were exposed to chemical and biological agents during Operation Desert Storm. Supporters of the veterans believe that the US was directly responsible for the weapons in the first place, having sold those chemical and biological agents to the Iraqi government.

In addition, it would appear that the veterans might have been used as test subjects by the military themselves. The military, it would seem, forced the troops to take injections of experimental drugs that were supposedly intended to protect them from biological weapons and nerve gas. Immediately prior to the Gulf War, the US Food and Drug Administration (FDA) adopted the Interim Rule, which allows the military to use experimental drugs on their staff without their consent "during times of military exigency". The Interim Rule is still being observed. As a result, the troops were given pyridostigmine bromide and botulinum toxoid vaccine. The FDA maintained that the military provided their staff with information about the side effects of these experimental drugs and demanded that thorough records be kept of the troops to which they were administered.

This, according to the National Gulf War Resource Center, is not the case, however. The Department of Defense (DOD) failed to inform troops of the possible side effects and virtually forced them into taking the injections. The DOD also failed to keep records of which troops were given experimental drugs and they did not keep complete records of the side effects that were inevitably experienced by the troops. This lack of record-keeping hinders veterans' ability to get medical help to this day.

What is most frightening is that the mycoplasma (bacteria) believed to cause Gulf War syndrome would appear to be highly contagious. It is claimed that some of the families of these Gulf War veterans have now been affected by the disease, and low-income families who were given surplus Desert Storm food at food banks may also have become ill.

Could this be a warped form of population control? Starting with men and women who pledged their lives to serve their country and who now can't get enough help from the authorities who sent them out in the first place?

After the 2003 Iraq combat, yet more US military personnel experienced similar symptoms, a factor which some have attributed to the US use of depleted uranium weapons during the conflict.

GUY FAWKES AND THE GUNPOWDER PLOT

On 5 November 1605, 36 barrels of gunpowder were found in a cellar beneath the Houses of Parliament in London – part of a conspiracy to bring down the English government and King James I. Although the plot was the brainchild of one Robert Catesby, Guy Fawkes was pegged as the mastermind of the plan, purportedly protesting against the religious persecution of Catholics in England. Theories concerning motives are widespread, but most historians believe that the plotters planned to assassinate the King, raise a popular rebellion and restore a Catholic monarch to the throne.

The full facts surrounding the discovery of the plot are unclear and a number of theories exist as to how the conspirators were foiled. Popular belief has it that a letter was sent to the Catholic Lord Monteagle, warning him of the plot and advising him not to attend the State Opening of Parliament. The suspected author of the letter was Francis Tresham, Monteagle's brother-in-law, who had been invited to join the "terrorists" but had declined. On receiving the letter, Monteagle allegedly informed Robert Cecil, the Earl of Salisbury. In the early hours of 5 November, a search party was sent into the Parliament cellars, where they discovered Fawkes and his cache of gunpowder.

One alternative theory suggests that Salisbury became aware of the plot some time before the warning was sent – the "Monteagle letter" may have been fabricated by government officials in order to frame the conspirators. After discovering the plot, government officials then let it develop, with the aim of catching the group red-handed.

A suggested motive for this conspiracy is that Salisbury wanted the King to come down more heavily on Catholics; by letting the plot continue he was able to foil it at the last minute and paint the Catholics in a bad light. It is also thought that he wanted to use the episode to increase his standing with the King by appearing to save his life at the last moment. Some even suggest that the whole thing was initiated by Salisbury himself, so that he had complete control over it and could ensure he was painted in the best light following his "discovery" of the plot.

One of the most convincing pieces of evidence for this is the difficulty the plotters would have had in obtaining gunpowder at a time when all stocks of it were controlled by the government. Salisbury, on the other hand, would have found it much easier to access stocks of the powder, which he could then have secretly passed on to Fawkes and the others.

Questions have also been raised as to why the cellars of the Houses of Parliament, which had never been searched by soldiers before, were suddenly subject to so much scrutiny – first Salisbury's guards and then the King's men. Why else would they have been searched had Salisbury not known about the plot?

The third piece of the puzzle relates to Tresham, who was found dead in his prison cell, having been poisoned. Was there someone who didn't want his secrets getting out? Was that person Salisbury? We'll probably never know for sure.

One thing we can be very sure about, however, is that Fawkes and his co-conspirators were publicly executed on 31 January 1606 at Westminster, outside the very building they had intended to blow up.

HAARP

Is the High Frequency Active Auroral Research Program (HAARP) a secret Star Wars-era weapon employed by the US government to influence domestic and foreign affairs?

HAARP is officially known as a project to study the effects and uses of the ionosphere, the uppermost part of the atmosphere, as a radio-wave-based surveillance and communication tool. It is jointly funded by the US Air Force, the US Navy, the Defense Advanced Research Agency and the University of Alaska.

Located in a remote part of Alaska, the isolated and foreboding-looking HAARP site is easily identifiable by the rows of mega-antenna pointing out toward space. For some, the programme has more sinister applications than those officially stated.

One theory is that the surveillance and communication-based research carried out at HAARP is just a small part of the activity taking place at the site and that the main focus of work has been the creation and development of a weather-modification weapons system. Theorists claim that the US government has used HAARP to destabilize their enemies and advance their control over the world's oil supplies.

Speculation has it that HAARP has developed technology able to create huge earthquakes and that it used this capability to trigger the Boxing Day tsunami in 2004. Why would it want to fake such a devastating natural disaster? In order to gain control over the oil-rich province of Aceh in Indonesia. What should be made of rumours that a 2,000-strong force of US marines was seen landing in Aceh immediately after the tsunami had struck? Was it to help facilitate autonomy for the province so that it could negotiate a lucrative oil deal with the US?

Others believe that HAARP lay behind the catastrophic Sichuan earthquake in China in May 2008, perhaps as part of an attempt to destabilize China's fast-growing economy. Office buildings in Shanghai's financial district were evacuated, as were a number of Beijing offices relating to the organization of the 2008 Olympics. Vital infrastructure, including airports and rail lines, was interrupted or damaged.

Another possible use theorists believe the US government may have for HAARP is to manipulate domestic policy; suggested examples include using the programme to accelerate the droughts that have affected the US's breadbasket and using HAARP to shoot down the *Columbia* space shuttle in 2003 in order to rein in the ruinously expensive space programme.

Then again, maybe HAARP is just a mind-control tool used to generate support for US government policies, or even a source of cheap electricity for the country's major oil companies.

HOLLOW EARTH

According to some, it cannot be doubted that Earth is in fact hollow and that there are people living inside, including descendants of survivors from the Atlantis culture. Those who adhere to this theory would have it that secret entrances are strategically placed around Earth, from which flying saucers emerge at regular intervals. In the middle of the hollow Earth there is supposedly a central sun, smaller than our own sun, but large enough to give light and warmth. This would explain the aurora borealis or aurora australis in evidence near the poles, said to be the sites of two secret entrances positioned where Earth's crust is thinnest. The central sun illuminating this inside world conjures up images of a tropical paradise; possibly the setting for the story of the Garden of Eden. Humanity, it would seem, originated inside Earth and then moved to the outside.

There are numerous variations on the theory proposed above. Some would say that flying saucers do indeed come from within Earth, but that they are not the vessels of the descendants of Atlantis, or even the proof of alien life, but rather that they come from secret bases built by the Nazis who discovered an entrance into this secret world just before the collapse of the Third Reich. Apparently they are still hiding there and are waiting for an opportune moment to relaunch their campaign against the outer Earth, having exterminated all the inner inhabitants who did not conform to their Aryan ideal.

Others would have it that the interior of Earth is inhabited, but the inhabitants are not physical in nature, so our normal earthly matter is no barrier to them. Or that the inhabitants are in fact four-dimensional beings, the extra dimension being incomprehensible to humans but meaning that they are only able to communicate telepathically with us. Some believe that there are underground cities, but they were not built by any advanced human civilization, but rather by alien beings from other planets that use the centre of Earth as a base. It's even been suggested that Earth is hollow, but that we are living on the inside without realizing it. The real laws of physics could be completely different from what we believe.

The most pressing question of all is how we could enter this hidden world. And that remains a mystery. Rumour would have it that Earth is shaped like a giant doughnut, with two holes at each pole providing an entrance into the inner lands. Others would say that the only entrance is through old tunnels, caves and potholes. Evidence would also support the possibility of other hidden entrances to the inner realm in Area 51 and other mysterious regions of the world. However, what seems most likely of all is that any entrance to the centre of Earth will have been hidden from view with the use of advanced technology that would prevent detection, as otherwise a giant hole would not stay secret for very long. This could be through the use of holograms, mind control or other psychological means, time travel, or methods not even imagined by our limited knowledge.

One thing, however, seems definite: the inhabitants of this inner realm do not want to expose their identity to us because if they did, assuming that they are aware of their situation, they surely would have done so by now. And if they do not want us to know of their existence, it does not suggest that their motives are entirely amicable. Whether governments have evidence of their existence or not cannot be proved, but governments that will not tell us what they do know about UFOs would certainly keep the lid on any information about people living at the centre of Earth.

There are some who even believe in the very real possibility of invasion and domination by these secretive inhabitants.

HURRICANE KATRINA

Hurricane Katrina hit the US state of Louisiana on 29 August 2005. It was one of the most violent storms the country has ever witnessed, causing the catastrophic flooding of New Orleans. The destructive weather front claimed over 1,800 lives and inflicted over $81 million worth of damage. But some would say that it wasn't entirely a "natural" disaster.

Certain theorists suggest that there was a human hand behind the devastation and that some of the 53 levees that were breached by floodwater in New Orleans were weakened intentionally by strategically placed explosives.

Islamic terrorists are among the accused. Was the bombing of vital levees a means of punishing the US for its War on Terror and historical abuse of power in the Middle East throughout the second half of the twentieth century? If that were the case, they acted with some success: the floods caused a high number of US fatalities and destabilized the George W. Bush administration's power base.

Or did a covert alliance of US government officials and industry figures orchestrate the collapse of the levees as part of a plan to raise oil prices? The Hurricane Katrina disaster brought to a halt a large volume of domestic crude oil and gas production as huge parts of Louisiana and other areas were evacuated, allowing oil prices to be driven up further. The close links of the Bush presidency to the oil industry are widely suspected.

Other sources say that the US government magnified the strength of the hurricane using secret weather-engineering technology, developed in collaboration with the Russians. What was the reason for such an act? It could have been to distract the nation from the news of fraud and bribery within the Bush administration that was breaking at the same time, which could have brought down the president.

Or was it to allow Bush to strengthen his martial-law-like control over the nation as he sought greater autocracy over domestic and foreign policy? This would explain why President Bush allowed chaos to reign in New Orleans for such a long period following the hurricane: the growing national panic gave him the opportunity to roll out stricter administrative measures. This illusion of command was intended to fortify his power base.

Another theory is that Hurricane Katrina was not a dark conspiracy, but was an act of divine retribution, reaped upon New Orleans in reprisal for its sins. Religious commentators lay the blame for the biblical-style destruction on the city's high murder rates, its liberal attitudes toward abortion and homosexuality, its history of witchcraft, and what they call its general immorality and depravity.

The New Orleans mayor is quoted as saying: "God is mad at America." Reverend Bill Shanks, a right-wing religious conservative, is credited as commenting: "New Orleans is abortion free... Mardi Gras free... free of the witchcraft and false religion. God purged all of that and now we start over again."

THE ILLUMINATI AND THE NEW WORLD ORDER

There are those who believe that a powerful group of individuals has been manipulating the course of global events for centuries as part of a plot to take control of the world and establish a New World Order.

It is alleged that this cabal was first formed by 13 genetically related families, or Illuminati, whose bloodline now reaches down every corridor of power. The world's richest people, most prominent politicians, most powerful corporate elite and highest-profile aristocracy, including the British royals, are all supposedly members.

What goal do they all serve? The creation of a feudalist state not witnessed since the Middle Ages, where the middle classes are vanquished and a class system of only rulers and servants prevails. This New World Order, or One World Government, would be stripped of national and regional borders, and would operate using a single monetary system. It would be policed by a One World Government force and a unified military. Only the subservient would survive, with the rebellious persecuted into extinction.

Another main aim of this fascist state is said to be a massive reduction in the planet's population, some say to as little as one billion people. The current size of the populace is placing a grave threat on Earth's natural resources and on its prospects of long-term survival. A large population is also said to pose a threat to the establishment and maintenance of control.

It is claimed that this New World Order has been behind most of the events in recent modern history that have caused colossal loss of life or have checked the power of other groups. The two great wars of the twentieth century, the Great Depression of the 1930s, the Korean War, the Vietnam War, the fall of the Soviet empire, both Gulf Wars, the Balkans War, the countless conflicts in Africa and the Middle East, the SARS and H1N1 pandemics, the Boxing Day tsunami and the 2007–2009 global recession: an invisible hand has allegedly been behind every incident.

Some say that this sabotage and manipulation goes back further still, even as far as the Crusades, which were supposedly triggered by a clan of Illuminati called the Knights Templar, a military sect of the Priory of Sion. The bloodshed and the lives lost over the centuries have all been part of a plan to establish a master race to control the world.

Today, theorists believe that most leaders of modern industrialized countries are members or are in collusion with this group, as are major captains of industry in such influential sectors as oil, banking and pharmaceuticals. Those who haven't been willing to cede power to this New World Order have been eliminated. It is claimed that the assassinations of John F. Kennedy and his brother were orchestrated by the Illuminati, because both represented a threat to its power base, while the Bhutto family in the Middle East has been a target thanks to the efforts of Ali Bhutto (the founder of the Pakistan People's Party) and, more recently, his daughter Benazir to bring greater stability to Pakistan. The deaths of other prominent figures who have fought for peace and whose ideals clashed with those of the Illuminati, such as John Lennon, have also been attributed to the work of this group.

But if all of this is true, how has the Illuminati managed to keep its presence and activities shrouded in near secrecy? Why has there been no popular uprising against such greed and power lust? A popular explanation is that the group has used mind-control programmes to keep society from mass radicalization, including the CIA's covert MK-Ultra project. Does the Illuminati keep a watchful eye over everyone and everything?

ISLAM AND EUROPE

The world has seen a lot of scaremongering over the years, and different groups often take the blame for the state of a society. One popular theory at the time of writing, and one that has been played on by right-wing politicians and media, is that Islam is taking over Europe. Certain newspapers run stories on how Islamic organizations are proliferating and diluting European culture almost every day.

Based on the idea that most of the world's terrorism is undertaken by Islamic groups, and that ever more Muslims are emigrating to European countries (although the official figures do not back this up), the more extreme theorists believe that the Islamic world has a militant agenda: to convert the whole world to Islam, starting with Europe. Recent "evidence" includes the increase in Islamic schools in the UK.

Aside from this, theorists cite news stories about European Muslims leaving their home countries, including the UK, to join ISIS (the Islamic State militant group). From their point of view, this could be seen as an attempt to build a new Islamic state in the Middle East, with even schoolchildren becoming involved. It is documented that Muslim extremists sometimes return to Europe from the Middle East, energized by their time away, to establish terrorist networks.

As this is reminiscent of Christianity's Crusades, and plays on many people's primal fear of things that are different and "other", perhaps this shows that history is repeating itself?

THE JESUS CONSPIRACY

Was Jesus merely a mortal prophet who was married with children, and whose bloodline survives to this day? Has this truth been suppressed over the millennia by ecclesiastical forces desperate to protect the power of Christianity and the church?

According to the Jesus conspiracy, Jesus was human, not an otherworldly figure who was resurrected post-crucifixion. It is claimed that he married Mary Magdalene and she bore him a child, or even several children, and that their descendants have walked the earth ever since. Furthermore, it is said that the Holy Grail is not the long-sought-after cup of a carpenter as is widely believed, but that it is actually Mary Magdalene and a symbol of the femininity that Jesus worshipped and which helped his Christian beliefs pass through the ages.

The theorists claim that these so-called truths have been safeguarded over the centuries by an ancient society by the name of the Priory of Sion. Members of this group have been mostly enlightened figures, such as Leonardo da Vinci and Sir Isaac Newton, both of whom are said to have been Grand

Masters of the clan. All members are dedicated to protecting this knowledge, chiefly against those equally determined to maintain the power of the Christian church and, in particular, Catholicism.

The followers of the Priory of Sion are said to have hidden clues to the existence of Mary Magdalene's marriage and motherhood, and the bloodline, in pieces of art, the most celebrated of which is da Vinci's *Last Supper*. Some claim that it is not Apostle John that is depicted to the right of Jesus in this famous fresco, but Mary, and that the "V" shape formed between the two refers to the symbol for femininity. Others point to the lack of a chalice on the table as further evidence of the Holy Grail's real identity.

It is supposed that the early church covered up the intimacy between Jesus and Mary Magdalene so that its teaching of celibacy would not be compromised and its misogynist power base, including the primacy of the apostle Peter, would not be threatened by women. In order to mask Jesus' relationship and procreation, and to maintain its control, the church cast Mary Magdalene as a prostitute and discarded any gospels from the New Testament – which forms part of the modern Bible – that spoke of her true status.

Since these times, the church has worked constantly to suppress these alleged truths, seeking to destroy the evidence that supposedly proves the existence of a bloodline and those who have proclaimed such events as truth. Is it not true that, if it were proved that Jesus was not part of a divine holy trinity, the church and its workings would be exposed as self-serving fraud? If that were the case, Dan Brown's best-selling novel based on this conspiracy theory, *The Da Vinci Code*, could be more fact than fiction.

JOHN F. KENNEDY

Who shot President John F. Kennedy, and why? Over 50 years since that fatal gunshot rang out from near the infamous grassy knoll, the debate is still raging...

LEE HARVEY OSWALD

The ten-month investigation of the Warren Commission concluded that the president was shot by Lee Harvey Oswald, who was murdered before he could stand trial. Thousands of conspiracy buffs believe that Lee Harvey Oswald was in fact put up to John F. Kennedy's assassination and then shot to stop him revealing the truth about what really happened. However... there is substantial evidence to suggest that Oswald *was* alone in shooting the president and that there was no conspiracy behind him.

If it was a conspiracy, it would have been, out of necessity, a more than superhumanly motivated team. For instance, how on earth could they have produced such a huge volume of evidence against Oswald in such a short space of time? They would have only had a matter of days to make their plans after the announcement of the parade route, and in that time they would have had to approach an assassin, research the details and plant strategic evidence – all without being discovered.

Oswald's actions themselves were distinctly suspicious in the week prior to the assassination. Why should he have made a midweek trip to where the gun was stored, the day after he heard about JFK passing his workplace, when surely the conspirators would have been able to do so themselves? And why should he have left behind his wedding ring on the fateful day that JFK was shot? And why should he have left work early after the assassination to wander around Dallas? Then, when approached by a police officer, why should he have shot him? All this seems to point to the resounding evidence that Oswald was himself guilty.

If a conspiracy was at work, it would seem that it was not very well thought out. Why, if there was a conspiracy, should the assassination have taken place in such a public location? If an organization such as the CIA or the FBI was behind it, then surely they would have had access to a more sophisticated means of attack. And if it was a conspiracy, why choose Oswald in the first place? The CIA, FBI, Mafia or military-industrial complex would have had a plethora of expert gunmen to choose from. If a conspiracy of such mammoth proportions was being mounted, then hiring such an unprofessional assassin would have been an unusual and unlikely move. Unless, of course, this very outlandish approach was intended to serve as a bluff and cunning cover.

The Warren Commission came to the conclusion that Oswald was the lone assassin and their verdict was based on witness statements, detailed films, photographs, more information on the autopsy and access to highly classified documents which we simply do not have. Conspiracy buffs, however, would counter this outcome by arguing that the Warren Commission was influenced by the government.

GOVERNMENT PLOT

There is the line of argument that the US government killed JFK. And why? One proponent would have it that 16 years after the Roswell incident, JFK wanted us to go extraterrestrial.

Conspiracy theorists state that the government had JFK assassinated in an effort to destroy the dream of space travel. Since the Roswell incident they had remained very mysterious about the truth of that day's events, thereby enjoying a measure of power over an ignorant and unwittingly vulnerable public. It follows, then, that the government would not be keen for society to learn the truth as a result of space travel, since whatever secret they had been harbouring would finally be exposed.

Ideas as to what this secret might be included the discovery of aliens who had already made contact with the human race, with whom the government are supposed to have made a deal: that the aliens could abduct humans and test them in return for advanced technology. Since the government wanted to keep their dealings with the interplanetary visitors under wraps, the theory goes, they had to have Kennedy assassinated to avoid him pushing ahead with space travel and making some startling discoveries.

It has also been suggested that Kennedy had already found out about the government's secret space missions, their deal with the extraterrestrials and a base on the moon housing up to 40,000 humans, as well as something sinister happening on Mars. The theory is that he was planning to go public with his discovery, so the government had to form an assassination plot before he did; they framed Oswald to avoid the suspicion that would have been aroused by a professionally organized killing.

FIDEL CASTRO

Fidel Castro, the communist leader of Cuba at the time, had previously shown much hostility toward the democratic US. When interrogated about the assassination, Castro denied any intention to murder the president, arguing that it would not be in his best interests at all, as such an action would provoke a US invasion against which he would have absolutely no chance of victory. Moreover, Kennedy himself had done very little to aggravate the Cuban leader. He had been very much against the idea of sending troops to Cuba, to the disgust of the military-industrial complex.

But even if he was not directly behind the assassination himself, it wouldn't have been hard for Fidel Castro or a colleague to investigate the background of Lee Harvey Oswald and persuade him to do it. Oswald was a communist and had distributed propaganda supporting the Cuban regime.

No one can know whether Castro would have wanted to do such a thing. He said that he was not unhappy with the situation and he knew that the chances of Kennedy declaring war on him were unlikely. Having said that, others would have dearly loved to force Castro out of Cuba. The US oil barons were one of the many groups who wanted him out, as he was destroying their factories and oil rigs in Cuba.

Kennedy had placed rigorous trade restrictions on the oil barons, thereby costing them millions, and with no attention being paid to this in the public sphere and no solution in sight, could they have taken the matter into their own hands?

The relations between Fidel Castro, Kennedy, the oil barons and Oswald are murky to say the least. But we do know for sure that there was considerable unresolved malaise. Could this have provoked one of the parties to murder?

THE MAFIA

It is a little-known fact that Kennedy's brother Robert was working to reduce the organized crime gangs of the US, including the Mafia. All the Mafia gang members had said that it would be beneficial to them if either Robert or John were out of the picture.

One could, of course, see the assassination as a severe warning to the US government to cut short their inquiries into the world of crime there and then. An assassination would certainly have been a dramatic way of proving to the world that no one, not even the president, could dare to tamper with them.

Witnesses claimed that they had seen Oswald on several occasions with Mafia gang members. And if Oswald had been working for the Mafia, could Jack Ruby have been employed to assassinate Oswald in turn to keep him from revealing the truth? Oswald had hinted that he knew more than he was letting on.

The Mafia's intentions were not peaceable. Constantly issuing demands for more weapons and men, they were outraged when JFK threatened to pull out of Vietnam. The US military presence in the country indirectly prevented the Vietnamese authorities from stopping a steady flow of drugs being smuggled into the US, which in turn boosted the Mafia's profits. When Kennedy was assassinated, the paper which he had drawn up stating that he was considering pulling out of

Vietnam was apparently lost – it would seem the Mafia had hit upon an effective solution for keeping open the flow of drugs into the US.

Could the Mafia have infiltrated the US government? Could some of its members have been bribed to influence the proceedings in which the Mafia were interested? Could this be the reason why there was never a full investigation into the possibility of a conspiracy?

THE CIA

Kennedy and the CIA had reached an impasse over the Bay of Pigs situation, in which Cuban exiles invaded Cuba in an attempt to overthrow Fidel Castro's government, aided by sponsorship and training from the CIA. The operation failed spectacularly, and the debate began as to who was responsible for the defeat. Neither side was prepared to give way. Kennedy blamed the CIA for mismanaging the invasion, while the CIA blamed Kennedy, accusing him of not having given them enough resources to work with. There certainly was a great deal of hostility in the air and even if the assassination was a more dramatic remedy than initially intended, it could have been the case that Kennedy had discovered a plot against either him personally or the government. Could it be that JFK needed to be silenced before he could say anything? Certainly one cannot rule out the possibility that the assassination was an act of self-defence, covering the intentions of the CIA. If it was to work, it would be essential to leave no trace behind.

And in this situation, it would have been imperative to use an outside assassin. The CIA could easily have put a threat on Kennedy's head, then Oswald could have heard all about it and then carried out the CIA's dirty work for them. The CIA would have had the personnel and expertise to cover their tracks and the very unprofessional nature of Oswald could itself have been a double bluff.

Moreover, the CIA could have used one of their secret service agents. Oswald could have been no more than the gunman that the public was meant to see. There are reports of agents on the scene that were not meant to exist. The theory of the second gunman could easily have been true. If so, could there have been an expert gunman hiding inside the grassy knoll?

THE MILITARY-INDUSTRIAL COMPLEX

Kennedy's plans to pull out of Vietnam certainly created much dissatisfaction, not only among the Mafia who thrive on war, but also among the military-industrial complex, the relationship between the government, armed forces and the manufacturing industries. The industrial arm of this Iron Triangle was already angry over his handling of Cuba.

Kennedy's re-election was all but certain and he had already issued a statement saying that once the elections were over he would pull his troops out of Vietnam. Yet just four days after the assassination, Johnson sent in more troops, totally going against Kennedy's wishes but delighting the Mafia and, even more so, the military-industrial complex.

The question of whether Kennedy could have angered the military-industrial complex enough for them to order his assassination is unresolved, but they were certainly unimpressed by his actions.

The other question is where the FBI comes into it all. It is unlikely that they would be considered as the assassins, only as conspirators. It is also dubious that they would consider such an overt action, as they tend to go for more secretive and less publicly orientated tasks.

But even if they were not directly responsible for the assassination, the FBI is responsible for the country's welfare, so it is possible that they would have had some prior intelligence of the planned murder.

THE KGB

Right-wing conspiracy theorists have it that Oswald performed the deed single-handedly all in the name of the communist cause. During the two years he spent in Russia, Oswald married a Russian woman, who was rumoured to have been under the influence of Marxist–Leninist supporters, and was indoctrinated into the benefits of the communist way of life. Moreover, the Cold War was at its most lethal and, when it came to it, Oswald seemed quite happy to do the honours, all in the name of love.

Professor Revilo Oliver wrote an account taking up 123 pages in the Warren Commission, and claims that the international communist conspiracy killed Kennedy because he was not serving it as efficiently as he had promised. Kennedy showed no signs of converting the US to communism. Oliver also concluded mournfully that, while Kennedy, a communist tool, was the object of national grief, not a tear was shed over the end of Adolf Hitler.

JOHN LENNON

John Lennon was shot on 8 December 1980 outside the Dakota building in New York, by 25-year-old Mark David Chapman. Was Chapman merely another disturbed killer, unsure of his own motives, or could there in fact have been political reasons behind the killing?

It would seem unlikely that Chapman killed Lennon to be famous. Over his lifetime, Chapman turned down around 40 interviews, and said himself: "I am not a seeker after publicity." He never gave an interview and never allowed documentaries which featured him to be filmed. Moreover, his composure after he had shot Lennon was quite remarkable.

Lennon was one of the most politically active musicians of his generation. This, coupled with his reputation as a drug user, classified him as an "undesirable" in the eyes of the authorities, making it difficult for him to obtain a green card to come and live in the US. The coinciding of his return to his former greatness with Reagan's rise to power is interesting to say the least. Reagan's policies were radical and Lennon was the only person who would have been able to bring out millions of people to protest against them. The question therefore has to be asked whether there may have been some kind of political involvement in his murder.

In the book *Who Killed John Lennon?* Fenton Bresler argued that Chapman was brainwashed and programmed to kill Lennon. Another theory goes that it was actually best-selling crime author Stephen King who killed Lennon and that Chapman was simply paid to take the blame for the murder. The theory highlights the physical likeness between King and Chapman, a coded government message allegedly hidden in newspaper headlines in the weeks before the murder and in letters written to the editor of a paper by people whose names, put together, include Chapman's full name and part of King's. One of the letter writers says that he is "a pawn just waiting for some giant hand to move me to some hostile square", and goes on to say that the hand is President Reagan. The theory suggests that this is a reference to government manipulation of Chapman in order to frame him for a crime that he never committed. In a strange twist, Chapman had approached King shortly before the murder to ask for a photograph of him and King standing together. He later claimed that he had originally planned to kill King instead but did not have the confidence, but it is possible that he was really meeting with the author to discuss their plan to kill Lennon.

KAREN SILKWOOD

Karen Silkwood died under mysterious circumstances in 1974. An activist and unionist who campaigned for better conditions at the Kerr–McGee processing plant in Oklahoma, she was on her way to deliver damning evidence to both a union representative and a *New York Times* reporter at the time of her death in an unexplained car crash. She was campaigning for health and safety issues, as corporate practices did not adequately take into account the safety of the everyday workers at the plant.

Had she not died in this crash, however, there is a high likelihood that Silkwood would have developed cancer due to radiation. During November 1974, tests revealed that Silkwood had levels of plutonium contamination in her body that were not consistent with her exposure at the plant. Her co-workers had much lower radioactivity levels, as did her housemate and her boyfriend. The suggestion was that, in fact, Kerr–McGee had been poisoning Silkwood intentionally as part of a plot to silence her.

KAREN SILKWOOD

Though liability was never proved, in 1979, a ten-month trial between Silkwood's estate and Kerr–McGee resulted in a payout to the estate of $1.38 million in damages, reduced from an original claim of $10 million. Public outrage about Silkwood's death and the circumstances surrounding it, as well as the aftermath, was widespread, as could be seen in the release of the 1983 film *Silkwood*, which starred Meryl Streep. Perhaps Kerr–McGee were trying to use money to cover up what they had done – we may never know.

KURSK NUCLEAR SUBMARINE

The *Kursk* nuclear submarine disaster, in which 118 people died, was an event widely covered by the world's media in late summer 2000, although most of the coverage of this tragedy focused on the unsuccessful rescue attempt and the personal stories of the submariners trapped under the Barents Sea, encased in a metal tomb. But was the disaster a simple naval accident or was there a more sinister explanation for what happened 108 metres below freezing Russian waters?

The five-year-old, double-hulled, Oscar-II-class submarine was part of a 50-strong fleet of warships involved in Russian naval exercises off Russia's northern coastline when two large explosions on board triggered disaster for the crew. The cause of those explosions remains highly contentious.

The official conclusion by the Russian government in 2002 after the raising and investigation of the wreck was that a faulty torpedo sank the *Kursk*, but theories about what really happened include that the submarine collided with the seabed, with a British or US submarine straying into Russian territorial waters, with an icebreaker or cargo ship, with an old World

War Two mine, or that it was an act of deliberate sabotage. It was claimed by Dmytro Korchynsky, head of the nationalist Ukrainian Political Association, that the *Kursk* was targeted by Chechen separatists. He also claimed that the Russian security services had been warned about this threat two weeks before but had not taken it seriously.

Could the true cause lie outside of Russia? Despite the end of the Cold War, British and US submarines have continued to play cat-and-mouse games with their Russian counterparts under the Atlantic Ocean. Naval crews on rival submarines often shadow each other's movements in these "games" but sometimes collisions can occur. Anonymous sources from inside the Ministry of Defence say that a British submarine may have been involved, but even if this were true the British government would never admit to it publicly. Intriguingly, on the day of the disaster the Russian national press agency, Interfax, reported that unidentified "military sources" had said that an object resembling part of a "foreign submarine tower" had been discovered on the seabed 330 metres from the *Kursk*. The same sources said the likeliest explanation for the sinking was collision with another submarine, "most likely British". However, this was vehemently denied by both the British and Russian defence ministries.

Senior Russian naval officers have their own version of what happened. They also believe a collision was the source of the disaster, but with a US submarine. They claim that two US submarines were conducting spy operations, and have produced satellite photographs of a US submarine docked in the Norwegian naval base of Bergen just after the *Kursk* sank. The Russian Navy insist this proves the submarine had surfaced for repairs resulting from the impact, since submarines are designed specifically to spend long periods underwater without the need to dock for supplies. In addition, photographs were taken during the failed rescue mission showing damage to the body of the craft consistent with theories of a scraping collision. The US Navy deny these allegations but, intriguingly, do admit to conducting operations in the area at the time of the disaster.

The most tantalizing explanation, though, is that one of the torpedoes on board the *Kursk* dramatically exploded, causing the devastating blast that was felt as far away as Alaska and measuring 4.2 on the Richter scale. Theories abound that a top-secret ultra-high-speed torpedo named Shkval was being covertly tested, a torpedo said to outperform any torpedo in the NATO arsenal – claims which would have heightened Russian concerns for security and for US spying operations.

Contradictory claims have also emerged with the release of secret British government documents involving a submarine accident off the English coastline in 1955. This involved the use of high-test peroxide to supply the torpedo's engine, which is thought to have caused an explosion. It was this danger which led to the technology being abandoned by the British but, perplexingly, it may have continued to be used by Russia and have been the major contributor to the *Kursk* tragedy.

In 2001 the communist newspaper *Komsomolskaya Pravda* suggested a cover-up by the Russian admiralty. It claimed a message was sent from the submarine to land-based commanders before the blast, saying, "We have a malfunctioning torpedo. Request permission to fire it." By denying this version, the Russian authorities conveniently detach blame from themselves, and from President Vladimir Putin, who was criticized for not cutting short his holiday during the crisis.

With all these various interpretations of what took place, the only consensus that has emerged is in the secrecy shown by all the sides allegedly involved. It is this sense of official denial and this hint of cover-up which generates the overwhelming feelings of injustice felt by the families of those involved.

KURT COBAIN

Was the premature and sudden death of the world-famous singer Kurt Cobain a simple case of suicide, or was his estranged wife, Courtney Love, involved in an alleged conspiracy that led to his death?

What seems strangest of all is the note left by Cobain directly prior to his dramatic exit scene. The tone was not typically suicidal, with statements such as: "I have it good, very good, and I'm grateful." The entire note was written in the present tense and seemed to be a far cry from the final words of a man about to kill himself.

According to psychologists at the rehabilitation centre Cobain visited only the week before, as well as close friends, no one suspected that he was suicidal – which, in light of his Rome "suicide attempt" (his overdose of champagne and Rohypnol a few months earlier), seems suspicious. Kurt had written Courtney a note after that incident which included one line which she said was "very definitely suicidal". "Dr Baker says I would have to choose between life and death," Kurt had written. "I'm choosing death."

There is the theory that Cobain was quite simply terrified for his life after walking out on a $9.5 million contract to headline the Lollapalooza music festival and that this inspired him to commit suicide. And the fact that the shotgun was loaded with three shells when the fatal deed was done could have been part of a plan to make his suicide look like murder. Strangest of all, police failed to find any fingerprints at all on the gun. Of course, perhaps Kurt had carefully covered his traces and wiped the gun down, but such behaviour is not what one expects from someone on the verge of suicide, and in any case, if it really was suicide, why the need for the big cover-up?

The fact that Courtney and Kurt were not getting on well before his death would seem little justification for cold-blooded killing. However, she could have had several other possible motives. In January 1994 Cobain told *Rolling Stone* that he might well be divorcing Courtney. Apparently divorce papers had already been drawn up by the time of his death, and it is believed that Courtney had instructed one of her lawyers to get the "meanest, most vicious divorce lawyer" she could find. Kurt had also hinted that he wanted Courtney taken out of his will, in which case she would have gained a lot more financially from a suicide before the will could be changed than from a divorce. If Kurt were to die, sales for his band, Nirvana, would rocket and Courtney would benefit financially.

The official line is that Kurt committed suicide by a self-inflicted gunshot wound to the head. In the days and weeks following his death, fans began killing themselves in empathy with their fallen hero. In light of this suicide rush, the backlash would have been devastating if police reversed their original judgement and opened a murder investigation.

THE LARGE HADRON COLLIDER WILL OPEN THE GATES OF HELL

When construction of the Large Hadron Collider (LHC) was completed by the European Organization for Nuclear Research (CERN) at the French–Swiss border in 2008, it caught the attention of many conspiracy theorists. The massive underground loop was designed to send particles crashing into each other at immense speed, allowing scientists to test various theories of particle physics. There were those who feared that, upon first being switched on, it would create a black hole that would immediately swallow up the Earth. Evidently, this did not happen, but as far as the theorists were concerned, the threat wasn't over yet.

Theories now began to focus on an even more sinister possibility: that the LHC would open up a portal between Earth and Hell. Fears about this peaked in June 2016, when photos emerged of an alarming lightning storm located directly above the LHC. Could this be an ominous sign that CERN's efforts to open a gateway to Hell (or some other hideous dimension) were finally coming to fruition? It just so happened to coincide with a peak period of activity in CERN's AWAKE (Advanced WAKEfield Experiment) project, the first run of which lasted from 2016 to 2018. Proponents of the Hell theory have pointed out that CERN forms the first four letters of Cernunnos, the horned god of the underworld in Celtic mythology, while others have used the fact that CERN has an on-site statue of Shiva, a Hindu god of destruction, to question CERN's religious affiliations: is it truly a scientific and neutral organization?

In August 2016 CERN was at the centre of a strange controversy, when footage emerged that appeared to show cloaked figures, gathered around the Shiva statue at CERN, taking part in a sacrificial ritual. It ended with a woman apparently being stabbed and the person filming crying out and fleeing. The video immediately went viral and conspiracy theorists held it up as evidence of CERN's plans to use the LHC to make contact with Satan. CERN's official response was that the video was a prank, and that it "does not condone this kind of action, which breaches CERN's professional guidelines. Those involved were identified and appropriate measures taken."

In response to the many theories and concerns about CERN's ulterior motives, and about the dangers posed by the activities of the LHC, the organization has created a special FAQ section on their website, in which they affirm that "CERN will not open a door to another dimension. If the experiments conducted at the LHC demonstrate the existence of certain particles it could help physicists to test various theories about nature and our

Universe, such as the presence of extra dimensions." Other concerns addressed in the FAQs include the fear that CERN is trying to prove that God does not exist; that shapes in the CERN logo represent 666, the biblical number of the beast; that Stephen Hawking predicted that the LHC will destroy the universe; and that the LHC can influence weather patterns and cause earthquakes and other "natural" phenomena.

THE LOCKERBIE BOMBING

On 20 August 2009, the convicted Lockerbie bomber Abdelbaset Ali al-Megrahi was freed from a Scottish prison on compassionate grounds after serving eight years in jail. Suffering from terminal prostate cancer, he was returned to Libya. Controversy and allegations of conspiracy surrounded the release from the moment it was announced.

Pan Am flight 103, destined for John F. Kennedy Airport in New York, was blown out of the sky on the evening of 21 December 1988, killing 270 people (259 passengers and crew, and 11 people on the ground) as the plane crashed on the Scottish town of Lockerbie. Megrahi was convicted of the bombing on 31 January 2001 and was sentenced to life imprisonment.

Many believe his release was approved not because of his illness or because of a prisoner transfer agreement between the UK and Libya, but as part of an oil deal involving the two countries. The UK's own oil reserves had shrunk significantly over the last decade and the country had become increasingly reliant on imported oil.

Was this alleged deal with oil-rich Libya engineered to help the UK become less dependent on Saudi Arabian and Russian natural resources? A relaxation of its dependency on Russian oil and gas would be a great relief to Whitehall as the Russian government has increasingly used this reliance on their commodities as a political weapon. Ukraine, among other countries, has found itself held to ransom over energy prices much inflated by the Russians, and protest over payment has led to supplies being cut off. An agreement with Libya would have allayed any UK government fears of being pushed into the same corner.

Others believe that then Libyan leader Colonel Gaddafi exploited the dithering over the Megrahi case between the London-based UK government and the devolved Scottish Parliament. This indecision, mainly concerning fears over negative public opinion at home and abroad, was allegedly pounced upon by Libya's ruler, who was well aware of the UK's need for oil and its desire to continue his country's rehabilitation into the international fold.

Sources say that Gaddafi warned the UK government of the catastrophic impact on the two countries' relationship if Megrahi died in jail. The angry reaction of the Libyan leader to Switzerland following the imprisonment of Gaddafi's son Hannibal and his pregnant wife in Geneva, for allegedly beating servants in July 2008, would have convinced UK officials that this threat was far from idle. Although Hannibal and his wife spent only two nights behind bars, the reprisals were swift and brutal. Swiss nationals living in Libya were targeted and arrested on spurious charges, trade sanctions were imposed, Swiss flights to Tripoli were stopped, the Swiss embassy in Tripoli was turned into a refuge for frightened Swiss nationals,

Libyan capital worth an estimated $5 billion was withdrawn from Swiss banks and oil exports to Switzerland were reduced.

Despite being in dire need of a major boost in public support, the UK government knew they couldn't risk such retribution. Megrahi was freed to widespread protest in August 2009. He received a hero's welcome on his return to Libya.

During the same month, an ex-CIA analyst claimed the CIA had a secret dossier which proved the Pan Am flight 103 attack had been orchestrated by Iran, and that it was to be presented as evidence in Megrahi's final appeal, suggesting that the withdrawal of the appeal to allow Megrahi's release on compassionate grounds was encouraged to prevent this information being presented in court.

Megrahi died in 2012, but there is no doubt that the theories surrounding his release, and whether he was guilty of orchestrating the Lockerbie bombing, will persist.

LONDON 7/7 BOMBINGS

Terrorism arrived on Britain's doorstep when four bombs exploded on London's public transport system on 7 July 2005, killing 56 people and injuring many more. The attacks were quickly linked to al-Qaeda but doubt remains over exactly who was behind these atrocities.

Three bombs were detonated within less than a minute of each other on three London Underground trains during the morning rush hour, resulting in a significant number of fatalities and injuries, while a fourth was set off almost an hour later on a double-decker bus in Tavistock Square.

It was widely reported following the attacks that responsibility lay with four Islamist suicide bombers, all of British descent, who sought reprisals on the British people for the country's involvement in the Iraq War. The nation was dumbfounded and it didn't take long for the media to infer a link to al-Qaeda.

However, as time has passed and new details have emerged, the official version of events has been increasingly questioned. Some theorists believe that the bombings were orchestrated by the British intelligence services as a means of generating greater support for the war in Iraq.

These people point toward the fact that there is alleged evidence showing that the bombs were placed under the Tube trains and not detonated from inside. One eyewitness is supposed to have been told to mind a hole where the bomb had been – the floor of the train had been pushed up and fractured, suggesting a massive force from below.

Special access to the Underground system would have been required to position the explosives and it is highly unlikely that the accused men would have been able to secure such admission. Were the suicide bombers just patsies set up to take the fall?

Then there are claims that the British government used an antiterrorist training exercise as cover to carry out the bombings. It is alleged that a UK crisis management company with links to the British state was running a training exercise in London that morning to test drills relating to terrorist attacks on the city, and that the British intelligence services used it as means of conducting their more sinister operation.

And what should be made of the fact that pristine identification documents belonging to the suicide bombers were found amid the wreckage? How could they have survived the blasts? Were they planted by MI5 agents after the event?

Theorists also point with suspicion to the fact that the British government announced that the bombers had travelled into London from Luton on a train that was actually cancelled. Had the plotters slipped up? Why were the CCTV cameras on the bus not working? Why did Israeli Finance Minister Benjamin Netanyahu decide to cancel a journey through one of the areas that would be bombed on that morning? Did MI5 forewarn the Israeli Secret Service, Mossad, about the bombings?

Others believe that the CIA carried out the bombings for financial gain. A lot of money was made on the stock exchange following the attacks, with individuals profiting from short-selling the British pound. The value of the currency, already sliding, plummeted further in the wake of 7/7. A similar pattern of events is said to have happened after the 9/11 attacks. There are those that say the transactions can be traced back directly to the US intelligence office.

MADRID TRAIN BOMBINGS

On 11 March 2004 at 7.39 a.m., a series of explosions hit the Madrid commuter train system. The bombs killed 191 people and injured 1,800 more. They also cost the ruling conservative party, the Partido Popular, its leadership of the country.

In the immediate aftermath of the attacks, José María Aznar's Spanish government firmly placed the blame for the bombings at the feet of the Basque terrorist group ETA, an organization which has claimed over 800 lives in its violent fight for Basque nationalism since the late 1960s. In the days that followed, the state maintained this belief despite mounting evidence to suggest that it was Islamic militants who had carried out the terrorist attacks. This steadfast reluctance to consider that the blame lay anywhere other than with ETA was very poorly received by the Spanish public.

Anger was such that the country witnessed mass demonstrations against the government. In a general election, held a few days after the train bombings, José María Aznar's pro-US government was ousted by a huge swing toward the Spanish Socialist Workers' Party led by José Luis Rodríguez Zapatero.

However, the al-Qaeda links have never been fully proved and theories remain with regards to the involvement of ETA. One theory goes that ETA and the Islamists collaborated in planning the attacks, timing them just prior to the elections in order to remove the pro-Iraq-War Aznar government from power and destabilize support for the Bush/Blair-led invasion. If this was the case, they were very successful, as one of the first acts of the new Zapatero government was to promise the withdrawal of Spanish troops from Iraq. Leading national newspapers continue to propagate speculation of ETA involvement to this day.

Others believe that the fact that many of the bombers were Moroccan points toward the involvement of the Moroccan Secret Service. Spain had forcibly retaken the islet of Perejil, situated off the North African coast, in July 2002, following an attempt by Morocco to claim it, and it is rumoured that lingering enmity over this aggressive action led the Moroccan intelligence service to withhold information that could have prevented the Madrid bombings – or even to collude in their orchestration.

More simply, the terrorist attack is considered by some as part of a violent and daring socialist party coup, with the Zapatero-led Spanish Socialist Workers' Party cruising to victory in the 14 March elections on a wave of populist support. The highly beneficial timing of the attacks for the main opposition party is an important factor for many observers.

MALCOLM X

On 21 February 1965 Malcolm X was killed by a shotgun blast at close range as he began a speech at the Audubon Ballroom in New York. On 10 March 1966 three men were convicted of murder in the first degree. One, Talmadge Hayer, a member of the Nation of Islam, confessed he was one of the gunmen, but insisted that the other two, Thomas 15X Johnson and Norman 3X Butler, were innocent.

The general feeling was that the Nation was behind the killing because Elijah Muhammad, the Nation's leader, had made it publicly known that he resented Malcolm's defection from the Nation and feared that he would reveal their secrets. One damaging secret was the allegation that the Nation had met with the US Nazi Party and the Ku Klux Klan and accepted money from racist whites – all of whom agreed with the Nation's policy of racial separation. Another secret was that Muhammad had fathered numerous "divine babies" with half a dozen teenaged Nation secretaries.

There are other theories about the assassination. One is that a narcotics cartel, perhaps Chinese, ordered the murder because of Malcolm's fight against Harlem's drug trade, which they thought had the potential to damage their business. Malcolm had previously given up all drugs and alcohol and tried to convince others to do the same, suggesting that drugs were one of the methods white people used to control black people – a claim that would have angered the local drug dealers.

Others maintain that the New York Police Department should be held responsible for Malcolm's death. They cite the existence of a second man who was arrested along with Hayer at the scene of the crime, who then mysteriously disappeared without having been named. He was not mentioned again in the press or police reports of the time, and some suggest he was an undercover police officer who was kept anonymous for his own protection. This theory is given strength by the lack of police security at the event; the 20 or so officers who were assigned to Malcolm's security were all stationed either in different parts of the building to the speech or even in other buildings nearby. The question is raised as to why they failed to provide effective protection for such a controversial figure – were the NYPD somehow involved in his assassination?

Another theory implicates the CIA and FBI in the killing. Malcolm was in the process of embarrassing the US government by accusing it of racism and human rights violations in Third World countries. A variation of this theory is that the government had Malcolm killed because he was moving away from racial separatism and was on the verge of becoming an effective civil rights leader, a movement which the authorities saw as a breeding ground for communist revolutionaries.

The real reasons behind Malcolm's assassination will probably never be known. His killing, like that of John F. Kennedy, will continue to be a source of conjecture for years to come.

MAN ON THE MOON

Did people from Earth actually travel to the moon? Some of the 500 million people who witnessed Neil Armstrong's landing on the moon on 20 July 1969 wondered at the time if something fishy was going on; could the entire thing have been an elaborate hoax presented by NASA, filmed using cinematic technology and created to claim the victory over Russia and other nations in the space race? The moon landings took place during a particularly unstable period of the Cold War, and it was thought that the first nation to put a man on the moon could use it as a base for nuclear weapons, so there was a very good reason for NASA and the US government to convince the world they had got there first.

Questions became more pressing with the release of the film *Capricorn One*, produced by Warner Brothers in 1978, which went so far as to record on screen how some of the effects might have been accomplished. The film showed a trip to Mars, cleverly faked so that the public believed what was happening to be real, which then led people to wonder whether the same thing had happened with the supposed moon shots of the late 1960s and early 1970s.

MAN ON THE MOON

Plenty of evidence is cited by those who don't believe the moon landings ever happened. Some point to the fluttering flag the astronauts were filmed erecting and ask how it could show these characteristics when there is no wind in space. Others claim that the different angles of the shadows on the moon – where the sun is the only source of direct light on to surface objects – were caused by studio lighting and are therefore proof of a hoax. Theorists also point to the lack of stars in the photos the astronauts took, explaining that stars should be clearly visible due to the lack of atmosphere on the moon.

For every hoax theory there is also a counter-theory, so perhaps man really did go to the moon. In that era's technological climate it would, ironically, have been easier to send someone to the moon and film them there than to attempt to reproduce the moon's environment on Earth. Even more modern films like *Apollo 13* had considerable difficulties in simulating weightlessness for shots of up to 20 seconds. The lengthy film material that was returned from the moon cannot be easily explained if it was a fake.

It would have been no mean feat to fake the launch of the enormous rocket craft, the Saturn V; again, it would seem to be far easier to actually execute the project than to perform such a massive illusion and somehow con the millions who were watching.

But this does not mean that all information we receive from NASA is exactly as it is portrayed. Even if astronauts did travel to the moon, did they find objects and structures that were never revealed to the public? Did they travel with ulterior motives? These theories are harder to disprove and knowing that we are only receiving information as it is filtered through the NASA censors is disquieting to say the least.

MARILYN MONROE

Of the hundreds of books that have been published about Marilyn Monroe since she died on 4 August 1962, around 50 are full-length accounts of only the last week of her life and the multiple conspiracy theories that have surfaced about her premature death.

The official ruling was that Marilyn committed suicide by an overdose of Nembutal barbiturates and chloral hydrate, but there are several odd details about the accounts of her death which remain unexplained to this day. The time of her death, for example, was recorded by those who found the body as between 9.30 p.m. and 11.30 p.m., but this was mysteriously changed at a later date. Her doctors and housekeeper were vague in response to questions and later changed their stories about the evening's events. Some of Monroe's friends were informed of her death at around 1 a.m., but the doctors later claimed that she hadn't died until 3 a.m. and the police were not called until sometime after 4 a.m. What is the reason for this gap? And why was the housekeeper allowed to leave for Europe soon afterward without being questioned again? The medical evidence was puzzling, too. There was nothing to suggest that Monroe had swallowed the drugs, so how had she taken them? It is assumed that she must have ingested them as an enema, which would seem an unlikely way to commit suicide.

On top of all this, the official verdict does not rule out the fact that there was a large number of people who wanted to be rid of her for one reason or another. If her death was indeed a suicide, it was undoubtedly very well timed.

Marilyn's affairs with highly placed individuals could have allowed her direct access to some of the innermost state secrets of the US. The CIA would be an obvious suspect in her questionable death if this was the case. If they discovered how much Monroe knew of their secret operations, the CIA may have decided that the safest way of ensuring she never let the information slip was to kill her, conspiring to make the death look like an accident to cover their tracks.

The Kennedys, at the time the most influential family in the US, also fall under suspicion. Her relationship with President John F. Kennedy is now well known, but at the time it was a closely guarded secret. Not only would Kennedy have wanted to keep the affair from public knowledge, but it has also been reported that he discussed highly classified secrets with Monroe; after he ended their relationship, he could have been worried that she would reveal his marital and political indiscretions. It has been suggested that the Kennedy family, relying for cover on their trustworthy reputation and excellent record of fighting crime, had Monroe killed (or even did it themselves) to stop her going public with her knowledge. This is given some credibility by the fact that Robert Kennedy is rumoured to have been seen in the area near Monroe's house on the evening of her death, although he obviously claimed her demise was nothing to do with him or his family.

The Mafia also come into question if rumours are true that she did know too much about a possible relationship between the Mafia and Frank Sinatra. Although the method of death seems a little unusual for a hired Mob killer, it is possible that this was a deliberate ploy to avoid suspicion falling on the Mafia.

There are also many who believe that Monroe's carers in her final weeks killed her for her riches, which could explain the sudden emigration of her housekeeper and the reported unwillingness of her doctors to divulge any information.

More disturbingly still, could Marilyn have been killed by aliens who were trying to cover up the fact that JFK was a member of a global unit of Freemasons bent on world domination? We may never know.

MARS

After Earth, Mars is the most habitable planet in our solar system and, despite now having freezing temperatures of around −50°C, research has shown that, once upon a time, the planet enjoyed a similar climate to our own. Studies suggest that all chances of inhabiting Mars were destroyed by a massive onslaught of comets and/or asteroids. The planet's surface is covered with craters as a testimony to this.

Photographs of possible microscopic fossils of bacteria-like organisms found in Martian meteorites have been unveiled, leading to conjecture that life must have, at one time, existed on Mars. Startling evidence has shown that intelligent life may have set foot on Mars at some stage in the past. Photographs of remarkable pyramid structures have come back from the planet, structures that seem not only to be artificially constructed but, moreover, bear a similar "face" to that of the Great Sphinx of Giza. The implications of this are quite staggering.

If the "pyramids" on Mars are what they appear to be, it would seem quite certain that they bear some link to the ones on Earth. Did an ancient, far superior civilization to our own go to Mars and build the pyramids? Or, more disturbingly, did an ancient civilization come to Earth from Mars and, in turn, build pyramids here? Or were the pyramids actually created by a civilization from another solar system, whose roots we cannot hope to understand?

A popular question raised by conspiracy theorists is whether or not investigations on Earth were carried out in a similar way to our investigations on Mars. In the long term, scientists are said to have plans for a series of experiments whereby, via the transportation of simple bacteria on to Mars, life could be introduced onto the planet. Nobody can disprove the theory that life on Earth was started in the same way. A more advanced and older civilization could have deliberately manufactured the way we live. If this was the case, further questions are prompted regarding the Martians' purpose or fate for us. Are we in fact the playthings of some mammoth intergalactic conspiracy?

Theorists also voice concerns that there are a select few here on Earth who know more than they are willing to share. Despite numerous missions to Mars, there are schools of thought suggesting that the images relayed to us in the media are nothing but an earthly fabrication, or, more worrying still, that the Martians have taken the explorers and are sending back only the images they want us to see.

MARTIN LUTHER KING JR

When Martin Luther King Jr was assassinated by gunshot in Memphis on 4 April 1968, there was outrage and a nationwide wave of riots in more than a hundred cities across the US. Two months later, escaped convict James Earl Ray, who had been linked to the crime when police found his fingerprints on a rifle recovered near the scene, was apprehended at London's Heathrow Airport after trying to leave the US on a false passport. He was extradited to the US and confessed to the assassination of King.

But how could a blatantly petty and inexperienced thief (his criminal career was typified by such offences as taxicab hold-ups and small corner-shop robberies, for which he usually got caught) pull off a complicated crime such as a high-profile assassination and make his way to London via Atlanta, Toronto and Portugal? How could he afford the travel expenses, much less plan the convoluted escape in advance? Congressional investigators estimated that Ray spent at least $9,607 between his prison escape and his London arrest, an amount roughly equal to over $60,000 by modern-day values.

And how could he concoct such an elaborate scheme, yet still be careless enough to leave the murder weapon at the scene of the crime with his fingerprints on it?

Days before he pleaded guilty, Ray expressed misgivings in a letter to his lawyer, Percy Foreman: "On this guilty plea, it seems to me that I am taking all the blame, which is all right with me." In another passage, Ray said, "It was my stupidity which got me into this." Memphis plastic surgeon Dr McCarthy DeMere, who served as Ray's physician at the jail, testified before Congress in 1978 that he once asked Ray, "Did you really do it?" To which Ray responded, "Well, let's put it this way: I wasn't in it by myself." Ray recounted his guilty plea just days after he entered it, saying that he had been talked into committing the crime. He was set up, he said, by a mystery man named "Raoul", who had recruited Ray into a smuggling enterprise.

Early in 1996, a woman named Glenda Grabow came forward, saying she had been carrying a secret for years. She knew Raoul. Her claim is detailed in a book by Dr William F. Pepper, who tracked the man and said the elusive Raoul now lives somewhere in the north-east of the US. But he is originally from Portugal, one of Ray's destinations on his travels between the assassination and his capture. Raoul was a weapons smuggler, said Grabow, and she claims to have seen him offloading and assembling illegal guns. Ray had said that he ran guns into Canada and Mexico for Raoul.

Ray's lawyer claimed that the US government was involved in the conspiracy to assassinate King. J. Edgar Hoover was outspoken about his distrust of King, accusing him of collusion with communists and calling him "the most notorious liar in the country" – surely reason enough to want to get rid of a popular figure? The FBI also had a low opinion of King, describing him as "the most dangerous and effective Negro leader in the country" and accusing him of taking advice from communists.

Those who believe in the conspiracy behind King's death allege that Ray was used as a scapegoat. He made his guilty plea under threat of the death penalty – if he had pleaded not guilty and been convicted, he would have been sentenced to death – and questions have been raised as to whether he would have confessed had this not been the case. He campaigned for a retrial until his death in 1998, and was supported in this cause by King's son, Dexter.

At a trial brought in 1999 by the King family against Loyd Jowers, who owned a restaurant near to where King was killed, Jowers admitted being paid $100,000 to arrange King's death and a Memphis jury found him guilty of the organization of the assassination and concluded that "government agencies" were also involved. Although a government investigation concluded in 2000 that there was insufficient evidence that either the CIA or the FBI had been involved, there are a number of other puzzling details that seem to contradict this. A fireman who was present at the time of the assassination is alleged to have told police arriving at the scene that the shot had come from a different patch of shrubbery than the police first thought, but he was ignored. A woman who also witnessed the scene reported that immediately after the shot was fired, she saw a man run away and drive off without the police trying to prevent his apparent getaway. Who was this mystery man and why were the police so insistent that the shot had come from a particular place, even though witnesses said otherwise? Were they acting on higher orders to allow a government assassin to escape? Or is the plot more complicated still?

Since almost every person allegedly involved in King's death has now died, it seems unlikely that a definitive answer will ever be reached.

MEN IN BLACK

The Men in Black have become a myth. And a terrifying one at that. Usually connected to UFO activity, the MIB seem to have developed a pattern whereby they will appear after any kind of extraterrestrial encounter and terrorize those unfortunate enough to have had such an encounter in the first place. The archetypal Men in Black are singled out by their black suits and tendency to travel in pairs in black cars, although they have been known to use the infamous black helicopters for transportation. Witnesses claim that they often look foreign, are abnormally tall and sometimes have no fingernails. Their spoken English has an indistinguishable accent, and they communicate seemingly without having to move their lips.

Jenny Randles records in her book, *Men in Black: Investigating the Truth Behind the Phenomenon*, multiple cases of MIB activity. For example, the case of Shirley Greenfield, victim of an alien abduction, is explored in the light of the MIB visitation that occurred shortly afterward. According to Randles, nine days after the abduction, two men appeared at the Greenfields' home, demanding to speak to Shirley and threatening to return later if they were denied access. The men apparently held a curious power over the Greenfields and displayed distinctly eccentric behaviour. Not addressing each other by name, they simply called each other "commander". They refused to say where they were from, refuting Mr Greenfield's assumptions that they were journalists. They appeared to be tape-recording the conversation using a square-shaped box, but one that was totally opaque, with no microphone, and whose tape did not need to be changed at any point during the proceedings. Randles goes on to show how they grilled Shirley aggressively about her abduction and issued her with a strict warning at the end of the conversation that she must not relay it to anyone. Wheedling everything that had happened out of her, the only thing that Shirley seemed reluctant to tell them was about the physical marks that the abduction had left on her upper arms. However, over the course of the next week, Shirley was plagued by telephone calls from the "commander", persistently asking her about physical evidence of what had happened. When Shirley finally confessed that, yes, she did have physical marks to prove what had happened, the interrogator seemed relieved and the telephone calls stopped.

The big question regarding the MIB is: who are they? Are they part of a government conspiracy to silence the victims of UFO activity? Is there an extra dimension that such activity has unearthed but one that the government is anxious not to reveal? Could this be a manifestation of the government's conspiracy with an extraterrestrial race, a conspiracy involving human abduction for medical experiment in exchange for technological know-how? Or is the mystery of the MIB more frightening still, and could they be from a power or force of which we are completely unaware? One thing seems certain: that they are prepared to go to any lengths to keep their identity secret. One can well ask what their motives are in doing this – and it would seem that if there were a logical, rational explanation, it would be out in the open.

MICHAEL JACKSON

Following reports of Michael Jackson's death from an apparent cardiac arrest on 25 June 2009, there was fevered speculation surrounding what happened that day at his Beverly Hills home and the UCLA Medical Center to which he was taken. Did he fake his own death? Was he already dead? Was he murdered?

Many people believe Jackson is still alive. The reason for the deceit? His disastrous finances. Despite selling over 61 million albums in the US alone, the troubled singer was reportedly in debt to the tune of more than $400 million at the time of his supposed death.

His spending had got seriously out of control (Neverland Ranch cost him an estimated $14.6 million in 1988) long before allegations of child abuse began to harm his reputation and stall his career. Huge lawsuit settlements and exorbitant legal fees took their inevitable toll on his fortune, forcing him to seek massive loans, initially from banks but increasingly from less salubrious lenders.

The theorists point out that faking his own death would have allowed him to settle these debts, while at the same time continuing to earn royalties, both from his own recordings (conveniently inflated enormously by his death) and from those in which he had a stake, including the incredibly valuable Beatles back catalogue.

It would also have provided a convenient escape route from what had the potential to be a catastrophic comeback tour in the UK. Few considered a clearly unwell Jackson able to fulfil a mammoth 50-date commitment. The embarrassment of having to lip-sync, looking decrepit on stage and cancelling shows could certainly have brought down the final curtain on his ailing career.

It is believed that Jackson fled abroad shortly after his reported fatal heart attack, with suspected destinations including Mexico and Eastern Europe, where he is said to have assumed a false identity, something which, in hindsight, he had been trying to achieve for years.

The change in Michael Jackson's appearance has been well documented and the acceleration of this mutation over his final decade coincides neatly with the time period over which the scheme had reportedly been in planning. It is claimed that Jackson was replaced by a terminally ill double, whose family is being looked after in return. Countless pictures and video clips have surfaced purporting to show the musician alive and well after the date of his death.

The Jackson clan's decision to cancel the public viewing of the body at the Neverland Ranch only gives further weight to the belief that the "Thriller" mastermind decided to stage his demise and live the rest of his life away from the pressures that had built up around him.

However, not everyone thinks Jackson is kicking back with Elvis in a private paradise. There is the theory that he died over 25 years ago, prior to the release of *Bad*, and that an impersonator took his place. It is rumoured that Jackson's body was found in a shallow grave near his miniature train track in Neverland. The authorities were tipped off to the corpse's identity as it was found wearing a single glove and a red leather jacket.

Another theory goes that Jackson's addiction to powerful anaesthetics, to treat chronic insomnia, was used as a cover by a shadowy group that sought his death. Made vulnerable by drug addiction and crippling debts, Jackson found himself controlled by a shady syndicate linked, according to different sources, to Russia, China or even the CIA. Attempts to free Jackson from their grip (most likely involving a threat to go public with the story), made by the singer himself or his family, forced the rogue organization to bump off their moonwalking cash cow.

Others believe that the Iranian politician Mahmoud Ahmadinejad sanctioned the murder of Jackson in order to distract Western media attention from the post-election chaos in Iran.

MICROCHIP IMPLANTS: THE MARK OF THE BEAST?

When the chip and PIN method of payment was first implemented throughout the world, a worried few voiced concerns over an imminent apocalypse.

It is not such a great leap to an age, much depicted by Hollywood, when we will no longer have to bother with PINs or passports. Everything about us will be stored in a chip the size of a grain of rice, embedded in our hands, where it can be read or traced through walls and over great distances. Just such an implantable biometric chip was implanted into dozens of employees of Three Square Market, a Wisconsin-based company specializing in vending machines, on 1 August 2017. There are obvious benefits to a chip system, but are we prepared to accept this loss of privacy?

Some religious groups warn that loss of privacy is the least of our troubles. Quoting the Bible, they warn that if society follows this invasive route, it will be an ominous fulfilment of a prophecy made a long time ago:

And he causeth all, both small and great, rich and poor, free and bond, to receive a mark in their right hand, or in their foreheads: And that no man might buy or sell, save he that had the mark, or the name of the beast, or the number of his name. Here is wisdom. Let him that hath understanding count the number of the beast: for it is the number of a man; and his number is 666.

Revelation 13:16–18

According to Tim Willard, managing director of US magazine *The Futurist*, everyone's social security number will consist of "a new, global, 18-digit mesh block configuration of international numbers that will allow people to be tracked internationally". Willard goes on to predict that this number will take the form of three sets of six: 6-6-6.

A further branch of this theory forecasts that there will be a single world government, divided into ten nations. One of these nations, the European Union, has already been formed, with a single currency in most of its participating countries. If we reject this "mark" it is thought that we will have no place in a soon-to-be-established new society.

Some predict that there will be no option – a few even suggest that a programme of compulsory identification has started, with the government secretly injecting the chips into people having routine operations or medical procedures. Certainly, chips have already been developed for some groups of vulnerable people considered at risk of straying from safety – for example, autism sufferers and people with Alzheimer's – so perhaps it is only a matter of time before a mass-chipping conspiracy becomes reality. Scientists and companies developing the technology claim that the benefits will outweigh the disadvantages.

On the other hand, the implementation could portend dark days ahead.

MK-ULTRA

MK-Ultra is believed to be a clandestine CIA mind-control programme. It was supposedly launched in the early 1950s and based on the work of Nazi scientists secretly smuggled into the US after World War Two; experimentation has apparently been carried out on unwitting citizens ever since.

The MK-Ultra programme was allegedly established by the CIA in 1953 in response to the use of mind-control techniques on captive US prisoners by the Chinese, North Koreans and Soviets. The US government also wanted to explore the possibility of influencing foreign leaders using mind control. It is said that Cuban leader Fidel Castro was an early target.

The science behind the project supposedly originated from research conducted by Nazi torture and brainwashing experts, who had been covertly transported to the US following trials at Nuremberg in 1945. This work helped further study into behaviour modification and interrogation, carried out under various guises – including Project Chatter and Project Artichoke – before a new title was coined for the experiments: MK-Ultra. The name is an amalgamation of the term used by the CIA to describe the most secret classification of World War Two intelligence (Ultra) and the prefix used by the agency's Technical Services Division (MK).

The main means by which the CIA supposedly sought to control the minds of subjects was through the application of various drugs. LSD was an early favourite and was initially given to so-called volunteers before being given to unsuspecting human guinea pigs. However, unpredictable results forced researchers to abandon the substance. Heroin, morphine, temazepam, mescaline and marijuana were also used. Hypnosis was applied as another form of control.

Soldiers are said to have been the subject of heavy experimentation throughout the 1950s–1970s, with drugs administered to make them both unflinching killing machines and impervious to torture and interrogation. It is speculated that the CIA trained assassins who could be put into a hypnotic trance, rendering them totally subservient to their masters' wishes but also incapable of recalling any act they had committed. Some say that the CIA used this practice to dispose of John F. Kennedy and his brother Robert.

MK-Ultra was first exposed in 1975 by the US Congress following investigations by the Church Committee and the Rockefeller Commission. Despite the inquiry, little was uncovered as it is claimed that the CIA, acting on growing concern over their activity becoming public knowledge, destroyed their files relating to the programme in 1973.

Many thought that this marked the end of the MK-Ultra project, but others believe it merely went underground and became an invisible CIA programme. Why would the CIA have turned their back on something that they had spent almost three decades and over $10 million perfecting?

CONSPIRACY THEORIES

One theory says that it was behind the People's Temple mass suicide in Jonestown, Guyana, in 1978, which saw 918 people take their own lives. Another has it that the programme was behind John Hinckley's attempt on the life of US President Ronald Reagan in 1981, a move fuelled by the CIA's embarrassment at an actor taking power at the White House. It is also said that Michael Jackson was a MK-Ultra slave and that his cosmetic surgery and increasingly erratic behaviour were results of CIA experimentation.

Others believe that the CIA was using MK-Ultra to control George W. Bush. His alcoholism gave the agency the perfect opportunity to implement their mind-control techniques; his decision to become dry provided a cover for the changes to his character resulting from the experiments. His subsequent embrace of Christianity was part of the alleged plot. The CIA was pulling Bush's strings throughout his presidency. The use of MK-Ultra could explain why Bush eagerly took the US into two wars where the chances of outright and long-lasting victory were slim, but the likelihood of bolstering the country's short-term oil supplies was high.

NAZCA LINES

The Nazca Lines have been a perpetual source of fascination for travellers for centuries. The lines appear in the Nazca Desert on a high plateau in the Peruvian Andes, 250 miles south of Lima. The thousands of lines resemble drawings of birds, spiders, lizards, apes, fish and other unidentifiable animals, as well as simple geometric patterns, shapes and straight lines. Many of the drawings are indistinguishable on the ground and can only be appreciated from the air. As the ancient Nazca Indians had no known method of flying it is unclear how or why they created them. Carbon-dating technology has estimated that the lines are at least 1,500 years old.

Various researchers have attempted to decipher these mysterious patterns throughout the ages. Many explanations make connections with outer space. Paul Kosok, a US scholar, tried to find alignments between the drawings and the stars to create an astronomical connection. It is believed that the Nazca Indians may have created the drawings as a form of worship to the gods, possibly linked to the natural world or to the success of their harvests.

Others believe the depictions weren't created by the Indians at all, and that it was visiting aliens who constructed them. Erich von Däniken published a book in 1968 entitled *Chariot of the Gods: Unsolved Mysteries of the Past*, where he put forward the theory that the lines represented a landing strip for alien spaceships. Von Däniken thought these extraterrestrials also constructed other wonders like the pyramids of Giza. Furthermore, a French book by Louis Pauwels and Jacques Bergier, *The Morning of the Magicians*, used the lines to advance their theory that aliens had visited Earth many thousands of years ago, during human prehistory. Through their highly advanced technology and intelligence, this alien species aided human beings in their primeval existence, enabling their superiority over other species and their takeover of the planet.

Some also believe that the aliens, who they allege made the markings, visited Earth to carry out a secret meeting with world leaders. The theory goes that they used the otherwise deserted area to land their enormous craft, travelled in secret to meet with the leaders and returned to the same remote spot to leave. The mysterious markings have been explained away by the governments involved to cover up the real reason for their existence. Some even believe that the extraterrestrials return on a regular basis, which is why the lines haven't been erased over the years – they are, in fact, fresh marks from recent landings. Another theory posits that the marks were created by humans with the intention of *attracting* aliens to Earth.

Others claim that the marks are nothing to do with aliens at all, but are instead evidence that the ancient Nazca people had developed some mysterious advanced technology. Whatever it was that made these marks, the theorists claim, other peoples must have become either jealous or frightened and destroyed it before it was put to its sinister purpose. Although there is little evidence for this theory, it does not seem impossible that these bizarre lines should have an equally bizarre explanation.

The strange markings are not alone, either. Further south, the world's largest human figure is etched into the side of Solitary Mountain, known as the Giant of Atacama. Elsewhere in South America there are many mountains with depictions of flying birds, spirals and ancient warrior-like beasts. With widely differing interpretations of their meanings, these mysteries are likely to continue for many centuries to come.

NAZI GOLD

The World Jewish Congress would have us believe that tons of gold stolen by the Nazis during World War Two are still kept to this day in the Federal Reserve Bank of New York and in the Bank of England in London. Furthermore, the organization claims that some of this may have been melted down from the fillings of Holocaust victims' teeth.

This is horrific in itself, but it is in fact only a subplot to a much more disturbing conspiracy theory involving the Swiss banks, which are alleged to have colluded with the Nazi regime. The Nazis didn't take over Switzerland and, in return, the Swiss took care of their bloodstained stolen treasure.

The World Jewish Congress has taken the situation very seriously ever since it transpired that the authorities in Zurich were hiding accounts of the Holocaust written by Jewish victims. It was later reported that the Swiss not only colluded with the Nazis during the war but, once the war was over, they also failed to return all of the Nazi treasure that they had been safeguarding.

While it would be shocking for a country that claimed to have been neutral to collude with the Nazis, it would be more appalling still if six tons of Nazi gold were to be discovered in the coffers of the Bank of England. A document from the US embassy in Paris stated that one post-war Allied shipment of 8,307 gold bars found in a German salt mine might "represent melted down gold teeth fillings". Although this does not conclusively prove the Nazi gold held by the Allied banks came from the teeth of murdered Jews, it certainly raises the question.

Another theory suggests a Mafia connection with the gold. According to this theory, Charles "Lucky" Luciano, a US mobster who specialized in illegal alcohol smuggling and gambling rackets, sent his associate Meyer Lansky to take a share of the Nazi gold. Lansky travelled to Switzerland and helped to transfer over $300 million into Swiss accounts, which he then laundered through other accounts until it was in the hands of his crooked bosses. This money allegedly helped to advance the Mafia's position into one of dominance in the worldwide criminal society. Lansky's purloining of this blood money and its subsequent laundering has never been proven, but the Mob certainly had contacts within Swiss banks and the know-how to carry off a scam of such proportions.

It has also been reported by various US intelligence sources that the Vatican confiscated Nazi gold to the value of around 350 million Swiss francs, at least 200 million of which is still said to be kept in Vatican bank vaults, mainly in gold coins. The Vatican denies this, but if it is true that they are harbouring gold stained with the blood of millions of people this must be one of the best-kept secrets in the world of conspiracies.

As for the Swiss banks, a compensation deal was eventually reached in which they were forced to pay out around $1.25 billion, but after 50 years this came too late for many Holocaust survivors and their families.

NEW COKE

In 1985, the Coca-Cola Company set out to make waves by introducing a new version of their ever-popular cola drink – they dubbed it "New Coke". New Coke had a huge launch campaign, and backing from Bill Cosby in its marketing, but despite early public acceptance of the product it did not do well, and the company quickly backtracked. This speedy reversal is what led conspiracy theorists to be interested in New Coke, and three of the most popular theories are mentioned below.

One theory is that this was in fact a huge campaign to increase sales. Essentially, the company changed the tried-and-tested Coke formula with the intention of upsetting consumers, so that they would demand a return to the old formula, causing a profitable spike in sales. The Coca-Cola Company's response to this was: "We're not that dumb, and we're not that smart."

A second theory is that the switch was simply designed to hide the change from using cane sugar in classic Coke to using the far cheaper high-fructose corn syrup, which would alter the taste, if only slightly. By using an interim product, the hope was that consumers would not notice the difference when regular Coke returned to the market. This is backed up by the fact that a US sugar trade association took out a full-page advert in which it berated Coke for using high-fructose corn syrup in the "old" formula when it was reintroduced.

According to another theory, the switch provided cover for the removal of all coca derivatives in the product for the benefit of the Drug Enforcement Administration, which was trying to stop production of the plant worldwide.

Whatever the truth, New Coke has become an integral part of Coke's history and legacy.

THE NORTH AMERICAN UNION

There is a theory that a mysterious group of elite globalists is planning to wipe the US, Canada and Mexico off the world map and create a new transnational state akin to the European Union. This is the North American Union conspiracy.

According to the theorists, the governments in Washington, Ottawa and Mexico City would be disbanded and replaced with a centralized European-style political system. How is this plot supposedly being implemented? They believe it is being accomplished by stealth: in the form of a string of free trade agreements.

The main features of the North American Union are a supposed colossal 12-lane superhighway and the deletion of national currencies, with a new communal monetary unit to replace them. The superhighway, or "super corridor" as it has been dubbed, stretching from the Yukon to the Yucatan, would be an intrinsic part of the new superstate, facilitating the easy movement of trade and people within its new, expanded borders. Many believe that secret plans have already been completed and are merely awaiting activation.

The North American Union would have a new currency, the amero, superseding US and Canadian dollars along with the Mexican peso. There is even talk that the English language would be dropped in favour of Spanish. The growth of the Hispanic population in the US into an increasingly powerful social and economic force would help facilitate such a controversial change.

So who exactly is behind it? Speculation has it that the North American Union is a concept created by a group of liberal industrialists whose corporations would benefit from the trade freedoms that such geographic expansion would create. Theorists argue that this clique is achieving its goal through an increasing number of bilateral trade agreements.

Are the activities of the North American Free Trade Agreement (NAFTA) and the Council on Foreign Relations (CFR) geared toward the realization of a North American Union-shaped future? Is it a coincidence that the CFR has produced a report entitled *Building a North American Community*?

Another organization that some believe to be implicated is the North American SuperCorridor Coalition (NASCO), whose mission is to support business along a trade corridor that stretches through eastern and central Canada, central US and deep into Mexico. It claims to connect 71 million people and underpin trade in the three countries worth $71 trillion.

Or is the North American Union a huge protectionist red herring engineered by right-wing business groups in the US? Some speculate that the superstate theory is part of a scheme to divert attention away from real issues facing the country, such as unemployment, illegal immigration and racial tension.

CONSPIRACY THEORIES

By playing on deep-seated fears over external threats, the propagation of the North American Union theory stops cohesive development behind improved labour rights, immigration reform, unionization and regulation of the marketplace, all of which would be detrimental to the corporate American right, which are opposed to the actions of such groups as NAFTA and the SPP.

NORTH KOREA AND THE US

With Kim Jong-Un proving himself to be an even more eccentric leader than his father, Kim Jong-Il, North Korea is very much in the public eye in the Western world. Outwardly, it appears that North Korea is the antithesis of the US, although Kim Jong-Un does indulge in Western frivolities. Some theorists, however, would have us believe that the animosity between the two countries is a front.

Instead of war being a possibility, proponents of this theory claim that the evidence proves the two are actually allies. This evidence comes in three parts: firstly, American basketball player Dennis Rodman's strange PR meetings with the dictator; secondly, the fact that North Korea's chances in a war against the US would be practically non-existent; finally, that a huge shipment of food was sent from the US to North Korea in 2012, even though relations were apparently already terrible then.

Though some might call this evidence circumstantial, there are those who strongly believe that the US is actually helping North Korea with its nuclear development, perhaps to keep some secret only Kim Jong-Un knows. One thing for sure is that, with the extreme measures this supposed cover-up has gone to, it is unlikely we will ever know the full story.

OKLAHOMA CITY BOMBING

The Oklahoma City bombing was completely bewildering, and the authorities have struggled to find some kind of motive behind the violence. Suggestions have included vengeance for the Waco Siege as well as an elaborate anti Bill Clinton plot, but the action would appear to be rather extreme if this was the case.

In a video lecture entitled "America in Peril", Mark Koernke stated that the United Nations had launched an invasion of the US, claiming that UN troops were pouring into the US and hiding in secret military bases. And the headquarters of these secret sites? None other than Oklahoma. Koernke also claimed that urban street gangs were being "trained, equipped and uniformed" to be deployed to the front line in the US invasion.

According to Koernke, the states of the US were set to be abolished and the country would be divided into ten regions under the iron fist of the UN. Moreover, as a part of their takeover plan, UN troops intended to lock up US citizens in 43 "detention camps" located throughout the nation. "And," he added, "the processing centre for detainees in the western half of the United States is Oklahoma City."

Newspapers reported that the executed bomber, Timothy James McVeigh, was one of several bodyguards for Koernke at a Florida appearance. If McVeigh and his co-conspirators were as close to Koernke as the press would have it, it seems possible that the Oklahoma City bombing was meant to be a lethal blow to the supposed UN plot to lock Americans into the aforementioned regional concentration camps.

In any case, it is perhaps difficult to believe that McVeigh and Terry Nichols, the other man convicted of the bombing, were capable of organizing such an enormous act of terrorism by themselves. Where would they have got so much fertilizer and racing-car fuel from, and wouldn't it have raised suspicions when they bought them? What would motivate two men to carry out an atrocity of this scale – surely not simply the anti-government message they were accused of sending?

Many theorists point to the examination of the blast site, and specifically the damage the building suffered. Several reports, including one independent report carried out in 1997, suggest that there must have been supplementary explosives within the building for it to have collapsed as it did. The truck bomb alone, claims the report, would not have been sufficient to cause structural damage on the scale that occurred. Analysis of nearby seismographs suggests that there were two tremors, which theorists claim proves the presence of another device already set up in the building. This alleged prior installation of a secondary device points to inside knowledge and suggests that there were more than just two men involved. Security cameras in the area also cut out shortly before the event, coming back online just in time to catch the blast – coincidence or the work of someone with expert knowledge? Perhaps there was a whole organization behind the bombing and the two men convicted were nothing more than scapegoats?

Some theorists say the group behind the bombing could potentially have had links to the very top – that is, to Bill Clinton, then president. They suggest that he may either have known about the plot in advance and done nothing about it, or even have ordered the whole operation in order to reflect badly on the militia movement McVeigh was accused of supporting. Although there is no evidence linking Clinton with the explosion, this would explain the supposed existence of the second device – who better to install a secret bomb than government agents trained to do exactly that?

Others feel that foreign influences may have been behind the bombings – Nichols may have come into contact with the man behind the World Trade Center bombing of 1993, and the van rented was from the same company used for previous truck bombings by foreign terrorist groups.

Although investigations repeatedly reopen into the tragedy as people stumble across more evidence of a conspiracy behind the bombing, we will never have a chance to ask McVeigh his side of the story, as he was executed by lethal injection in 2001.

THE ORDER OF SKULL AND BONES

Prophecies of a New World Order have been made for centuries and never quite come to fruition – or at least not explicitly. From the Illuminati to the Bilderbergs, secret Masonic-style cliques have been rumoured to be controlling or seeking to control the direction of world events.

The Order of Skull and Bones is a secret society based at Yale University in the US, for the males of prominent families. Its most famous past members allegedly include former US president George W. Bush and his father and former president George H. W. Bush. The group's activities are not known publicly but rumours abound of clandestine plots to reshape the global order and to influence political figures and institutions. Former members have gone on to become senators, Supreme Court justices and ambassadors, as well as three becoming president. Other famous people who are said to have been through the society include members of the Rockefeller, Pillsbury and Taft families.

Initially the society was formed to benefit members when they left college, in a similar manner to the way the Freemasons group together to share ideals, financial interests and assistance. But former Bones members have been accused of creating a secret government under the guise of intelligence operations, sometimes working against the interests of the president and carrying out operations in his name. Some of the most famous US scandals have the fingerprints of Bones alumni all over them, from the assassination of JFK to Watergate and the Iran–Contra scandal. The person some claim had a hand in all of these events is George H. W. Bush. At the time of the JFK assassination and the Watergate break-in Bush was working for the CIA, and during the Iran–Contra affair he was vice president.

The influence of former members of this secret society upon US political life takes President Dwight D. Eisenhower's warnings about the corruption of power within the military-industrial complex to a whole new level. It was allegedly Eisenhower himself who created this "secret government" under the guise of intelligence operations, a group which conducts its activities in secret for "national security". He appointed to Gordon Gray the task of hiding these activities. Gray's son, C. Bowden, was George H. W. Bush's White House counsel and "protector of the president, come what may". His job was to ensure that Bush was not implicated in the group's activities if any of this became public. Allegations against this secret group include drug trafficking under the veil of the war on drugs, financing communism and funding Hitler's regime.

But one of the most intriguing aspects is that the two major candidates in the 2004 US presidential election, George W. Bush and John Kerry, were both former Bones members.

Both men were believed to have been in the pockets of the Bones' guiding fathers, so that whoever won, the society's hold over the centre of power would be assured for the next four years. Furthermore, John Kerry's wife Teresa was previously married to John Heinz, another Yale alumnus and Bones member. Heinz was also an outspoken liberal, often voicing opinions that were not compatible with those of the government. More interestingly, he was part of the commission that looked into the Iran–Contra scandal along with John Tower. Both men saw reams of classified information that implicated the CIA in illegal activity while George H. W. Bush was their director. The two men curiously perished in mysterious plane crashes on successive days in 1991.

Could it be that the Skull and Bones society have exerted their influence over the White House for decades, and not only have the ear of the president but are controlling his voice and actions too? Without any accountability to the US people, it could be these behind-the-scenes puppeteers who are really pulling the strings. Although the Bonesmen's grip on the presidency appeared to loosen during Obama's time in office, some of his key advisors were discovered to have been former Bonesmen, and theorists claim that the secret government still retain their power despite the best efforts of those ostensibly in charge.

OSAMA BIN LADEN'S ASSASSINATION WAS A HOAX

On 2 May 2011, Osama Bin Laden was killed at his secret hideout in Abbottabad, Pakistan, in a United States Navy Seals operation codenamed Operation Neptune Spear. Or was he?

There has been much controversy and many conspiracy theories surrounding the assassination of the infamous al-Qaeda leader, including those alleging that he wasn't killed at all that day. Proponents of this theory point to the following as causes for suspicion: the US military supposedly disposed of the body at sea; no photographic or DNA evidence of bin Laden's death was released to the public; there were various contradictory accounts of the raid; and there was a 25-minute blackout during the operation when the live feed was cut from cameras mounted on the helmets of the US special forces personnel.

Rumours circulated on the internet that the raid and killing were faked in an attempt to create a distraction from questions about President Obama's citizenship, or even to boost Obama's popularity during the 2012 election. Some theorists, including Hamid Gul, the former head of Pakistan's Inter-Services Intelligence, even suggested that Bin Laden had already been dead for years. Others agreed that Bin Laden had been killed a number of years ago, and that it had been kept secret to ensure continued support for the War on Terror.

Could it also have been the case that the announcement of Bin Laden's assassination was timed to conflict with and take Donald Trump's *Celebrity Apprentice* off the air, to punish Trump for questioning the authenticity of Barack Obama's birth certificate? Or was the announcement about his death even delayed so as not to clash with the royal wedding in England of Prince William and Catherine Middleton?

OSCAR PISTORIUS

Famous for his incredible sprinting skills using "blade" prosthetics, double-amputee Oscar Pistorius was a celebrated Paralympian until accused of murdering his girlfriend in cold blood.

Reeva Steenkamp was shot by Pistorius through the bathroom door of his luxury home in Pretoria. He claimed that, hearing noises in the night, he had assumed there was an intruder in the house and had therefore armed himself. He fired the gun believing that the person on the other side of the door was a stranger who had broken into his home – believing he was defending himself and, by proxy, Steenkamp.

Just the basics of this story would seem questionable to even the lay reader, and the court is said to have seen the tale as just that, but somehow Pistorius was convicted of culpable homicide, the South African equivalent of manslaughter, not of murder. Theorists have it that Pistorius' "luck" in being charged with a lesser crime came down to protection from the ever-present Illuminati. Some believe that Pistorius became a member and was therefore invulnerable – no jury could return a guilty verdict on murder due to the influence of the Illuminati.

Further, some have it that the prosecution failed to look into the astrological reasoning, known as astropsychology and astroforensics, behind Pistorius' actions, stating that the planetary alignments at the time of the shooting are proof of his culpability but that this was ignored.

However, Pistorious's luck (or protection?) was not to last. In 2015 the Supreme Court of Appeal overturned the culpable homicide verdict and convicted him of murder, and Judge Thokozile Masipa extended the sentence to six years. A subsequent appeal by the state saw his sentence doubled to 13 years and five months. Surely if the Illuminati truly were involved, Pistorius would have only had to serve the original sentence?

PAUL WELLSTONE

On 25 October 2002 Paul Wellstone, a progressive US senator, was killed when his private jet crashed into the ground and burst into flames two miles short of its destination in Minnesota. Reports initially suggested that mechanical failure was to blame for the disaster, but some believe that Wellstone was the victim of a political assassination. Never shy to voice his opinions, the liberal Democrat was a well-publicized opponent of George W. Bush's plans to go to war with Iraq again; the only senator, in fact, to vote against it.

Investigators concluded that none of the typical causes of a small plane accident – engine failure, icing or pilot error – caused the plane to crash. And while weather conditions were less than ideal, with some ice and freezing rain, visibility was well above the minimum required (around 3–4 kilometres). Although the approach to the airport was made using instruments, the airport would have been in clear view of the pilot once he descended beneath the lowest cloud layer at about 210 metres.

Under different political circumstances one would dismiss Wellstone's death as a tragic accident whose cause, even if it cannot be precisely determined, lies in the sphere of aircraft engineering and weather phenomena. But, interestingly, Wellstone's death came almost two years to the day after a similar plane crash killed a Democratic senate hopeful, Missouri Governor Mel Carnahan, on 16 October 2000.

PEAK OIL

The term "peak oil" refers to the point in time when worldwide oil production reaches its maximum level, after which the rate of extraction enters a decline that ends in exhaustion. It has come under scrutiny, with some theorists claiming that it is a concept propagated by an elite group of politicians, rulers and oil industry figures to create a state of artificial scarcity and increase commodity prices.

Theorists who take this view point toward supposed scientific evidence that oil is actually an infinite resource, as well as alleged leaked confidential memos from oil industry companies and inconsistent data from key production sites, as proof of a conspiracy. They believe that it has been created by this powerful bloc to maintain their hold over a populace made subservient by dependency on oil and to keep their pockets lined.

What should we make of scientific evidence presented by theorists that claim oil is a renewable abiotic and not a finite source produced from long-decayed biological matter? If the planet was found to be replenishing stocks of oil, wouldn't the power and riches of the world's major oil-producing countries and companies be much diluted? Back these powerful players into a corner and what are they going to do? Protect themselves and their bottom lines, that's what.

Cynics also point to the mysterious fluctuations in production at the Eugene Island 330 oil field in the Gulf of Mexico. Discovered in 1973, the site initially yielded 15,000 barrels a day before the rate slowed to 4,000 barrels in 1989. However, output later returned to a level of 13,000 barrels a day. What was behind the changing figures? Does it mean that this field is refilling itself, thus blowing the peak oil theory – supported by the likes of OPEC (the Organization of the Petroleum Exporting Countries), the IMF (International Monetary Fund), and countless major governments and oil conglomerates – out of the water?

There has been speculation that the oil companies themselves knew the peak oil theory to be fraudulent. Theorists claim to have seen notes outlining strategies to deliberately create artificial scarcity and inflate prices from Mobil, Chevron and Texaco. A Chevron memo is said to have circulated a warning against the impact on margins of continuing high levels of extraction.

The second war against Iraq is widely accused of being an invasion based on oil. Was the US government, led by George W. Bush and his oil-industry-linked bunch of cronies, just taking the opportunity to seize further control over the world's oil resources, giving all those involved even greater power in a consumer environment made fearful and compliant by the peak oil theory? Was this the reason that this administration worked so hard to suppress alternative fuel technologies?

PEAK OIL

Oil companies, governments and major global organizations have all gone to great lengths to debunk these theories, but the discovery of huge oil reserves by British Petroleum in the Gulf of Mexico in September 2009, and Iran's announcement of an even larger find of over 50 billion barrels in 2019, casts doubt over the certainties propagated by those with the most to lose if oil is found to be more plentiful than expected. These oil discoveries, along with others in Uganda, western Greenland and Brazil, all contribute to the counter-theory that peak oil is a pack of lies.

PEARL HARBOR

One of the defining moments of World War Two was the Japanese "surprise" attack on Pearl Harbor, which brought the US into the war. Without this attack and without US involvement in Western Europe, the shape of the post-war world may well have been entirely different.

But was the attack on Pearl Harbor in December 1941 really a surprise? Theorists have come up with evidence suggesting that President Franklin D. Roosevelt knew about the planned attack and kept it secret to promote his wartime ambitions. Roosevelt was keen to involve the US in the war in Western Europe but was restrained by public opinion, which ran at 88 per cent against joining the Allies. In addition, he had promised during his re-election campaign: "I have said this before, but I shall say it again and again and again: your boys are not going to be sent into any foreign wars." However, in private Roosevelt planned for US troops to go to war to help fight for freedom.

In the months and years leading up to the attack, the US had continuously provoked Japan by freezing its assets, halting exports, employing an embargo and refusing access to the Panama Canal for Japanese ships. In his war diary of 16 October 1941, Secretary of War Henry Stimson wrote: "We face the delicate question of the diplomatic fencing to be done so as to be sure Japan is put into the wrong and makes the first bad move – overt move." A month later he wrote: "The question was how we should manoeuvre them [the Japanese] into the position of firing the first shot."

The theory goes that the commanders at Pearl Harbor were not made aware of the vital intelligence being gleaned in Washington. Of greatest importance was Washington's ability to crack Japan's secret diplomatic code, known as "Purple". This highly encrypted code was cracked by US signals intelligence in 1940 and was used to read Japanese diplomatic communications. Copies of this intelligence were not passed to commanders at Pearl Harbor, however, despite its obvious vulnerability to attack and complaints from the armed forces based there. An interception made on 11 November is said to have warned: "The situation is nearing a climax, and the time is getting short."

Equally, when the Japanese naval fleet approached Hawaii, it has always been claimed that it had complete radio silence, making it undetectable. But theorists cite the following interception, allegedly made from a dispatch from Admiral Yamamoto to the Japanese First Air Fleet on 26 November 1941: "The task force, keeping its movement strictly secret and maintaining close guard against submarines and aircraft, shall advance into Hawaiian waters, and upon the very opening of hostilities shall attack the main force of the US fleet and deal it a mortal blow. The first air raid is planned for the dawn of x-day. Exact date to be given by later order." These clear warnings were never acted upon by the US Navy, in a chain of command that led ultimately to the president. Despite repeated warnings from Dutch, Korean and British agents about a possible attack, the US government either showed incredible ineptitude or deliberately overlooked the threat.

As further evidence, theorists maintain that all merchant shipping in the Western Pacific was halted on the day of the attack, presumably to avoid the Japanese fleet being spotted and the alarm being raised, which would have ruined FDR's careful planning.

The commission that looked into the attacks was undertaken by cronies loyal to Roosevelt, who decided that the attacks were a "dereliction of duty" by the Hawaiian commanders; the same commanders to whom Washington had denied intelligence briefings. With public anger directed toward them and Japan, the real culprits were allowed to proceed with their previously unpopular war plan.

THE PHANTOM TIME HYPOTHESIS

According to this hypothesis, which has been put forward by German historian Heribert Illig and taken up by many conspiracy theorists, the year 613 was followed directly by the year 911, and events between 614–911 have either been wrongly dated or did not happen at all – a fact which there has been a systematic effort to cover up.

The apparent reason for this is a conspiracy between Holy Roman Emperor Otto III, Pope Sylvester II, and perhaps also the Byzantine Emperor Constantine VII, who wanted to change the dating system so that they would be placed as central figures at the millennium. To do this involved rewriting history – including, apparently, inventing Charlemagne.

There is a great deal of proof to support this hypothesis. Firstly, and coupled with the over-reliance of medieval historians on written sources, there is no real archaeological evidence that can be reliably dated to the period 614–911.

Perhaps the strongest argument for this theory, though, is the relationship between the Julian and Gregorian calendars, and the underlying solar (tropical) year. The Julian calendar was known to introduce a difference from the tropical year of around one day per century. By the time the Gregorian calendar was introduced, in 1582, the Julian calendar should have created a discrepancy of 13 days. Instead only ten days needed to be introduced, suggesting that around three centuries had, in fact, never existed.

Though there are arguments against this theory, such as observations in ancient Chinese astronomy and the apparent lack of fabrication in the rest of the world's history, the "phantom time" would certainly explain why the era in question is known as the Dark Ages!

PHARMACEUTICAL COMPANIES

Pharmaceutical companies are among the world's largest corporations, and every human being is dependent on the medicines they produce, from aspirin and cold remedies to treatments for diabetes and cancer. The relationship is a simple case of supply and demand. Or is it?

Many believe that pharmaceutical companies are a malevolent force in global healthcare that perpetuate the consumption of expensive drugs over less costly treatments. The reports of price fixing and illegal marketing involving the sector's major manufacturers are just the tip of the iceberg. These are activities that the companies are more or less content to admit to – the fines are a small price to pay for the cover that paying them provides.

Some "Big Pharma" theorists suggest that the drug industry controls every healthcare system in the world and they use this unprecedented power base to replace natural, non-patentable medicines with man-made alternatives whose high prices line their already deep pockets. It is claimed that pharmaceutical companies have suppressed, or are holding back, cures for cancer, diabetes, the HIV virus, and several other virulent infectious diseases that have caused so much hysteria in the last few decades. Why have they done this? Is it because they are fearful of the damage such medicines would do to their profits?

At the same time as suppressing discoveries, it is said that drug manufacturers also work to maintain the high incidence of diseases in society. By making sure that their drugs do not provide a cure for illnesses, and in some cases generate new strains of diseases, they are guaranteeing a continuous revenue stream. Why would these multibillion dollar companies want to threaten such a lucrative trade? What should be made of the alleged accidental release of a contaminated batch of H1N1 flu virus treatments, which were capable of spreading the virus, by a US drug company? Is it an example of more disease cases, more money?

According to one theory, it is not just capitalist greed behind this alleged scheming, but a plan to take over the world. This view suggests that the people in control of the world's major drug companies belong to a clandestine cabal who are intent on installing a One World Government, a fascist state ruled by the elite, whose population is subservient to the needs of the master race. The continued prevalence of diseases – debilitating, deadly or otherwise – is a means of financing this revolution and keeping the general populace de-radicalized and enslaved.

PIZZAGATE

What do child-sex traffickers and pizza makers have in common? Nothing, you might think. And yet a virulent conspiracy theory connected the two, leading to an explosive and shocking incident.

In 2016, Hillary Clinton's campaign manager, John Podesta, was the target of a spear-phishing attack. WikiLeaks obtained and published 20,000 emails allegedly from Podesta in November that year. Most people who read the emails focused on the insight they gave into the inner workings of the Clinton campaign: for example, they gave rise to the suggestion that CNN commentator Donna Brazile shared audience questions with the Clinton campaign in advance of town hall meetings. But others who read the emails homed in on what they claimed to be coded messages that connected high-ranking officials in the Democratic Party with a human trafficking and child-sex ring.

One of the emails was allegedly between Podesta and James Alefantis, the owner of the Comet Ping Pong pizzeria in Washington D.C., and made reference to the possibility of

Alefantis hosting a fundraiser for Clinton. Theorists began to speculate about the link between Comet Ping Pong and the Democratic Party on the website 4Chan, culminating in the conclusion that Comet Ping Pong was the base for a child-abuse ring led by Hillary Clinton.

The story gained traction and was posted on sites such as Your News Wire, The New Nationalist, The Vigilant Citizen and the pro-Trump SubjectPolitics.com. Soon it had gone viral on social media with the hashtag #pizzagate, and Alefantis and his staff became the target of online abuse and threats. One message even read, "I will kill you personally," according to *The New York Times*. From there it continued to escalate. Photos of customers' children were even taken from the restaurant's social media and used in articles as "evidence" of the child-abuse ring.

Then, on 4 December 2016, things came to a head when 28-year-old Edgar Maddison Welch, of Salisbury, North Carolina, walked into Comet Ping Pong holding an assault rifle and threatened an employee with it. The employee managed to get away and called the police. Welch fired his gun, possibly striking the walls, door and a computer. Luckily, no one was hurt. Police surrounded the restaurant and arrested Welch, who said he had gone there to "self-investigate" reports of a child-trafficking ring.

Although Alefantis was a Clinton supporter, he had never met her, though it's true that he did have some links to the Democratic Party: Tony Podesta, brother of John Podesta, frequented the restaurant, and Alefantis was at one time in a relationship with David Brock, described by the *New York Times* as "a provocative former right-wing journalist who became an outspoken advocate for Mrs Clinton".

PIZZAGATE

Alefantis argues that the child-trafficking accusations are nothing more than fake news. After the shooting incident, he made the following statement:

> *What happened today demonstrates that promoting false and reckless conspiracy theories comes with consequences. I hope that those involved in fanning these flames will take a moment to contemplate what happened here today, and stop promoting these falsehoods right away.*

The pizzagate conspiracy theory continued to rumble on for some time after the shooting, but it has since been widely discredited and debunked by various sources, including *The New York Times, The Washington Post* and *The Independent*.

POPE JOHN PAUL I

Pope John Paul I died in mysterious circumstances after just 33 days in office. But was anyone behind the new pope's untimely death?

To appreciate the possible causes behind the demise of Pope John Paul I it is necessary to refer to the religious ructions that occurred during the nineteenth century when the Catholic Church was stripped of its powers in the Italian national revolution of 1848. Pope Pius IX, then in power, compensated for his loss of earthly land and power by ordering the Vatican Council to pass the doctrine of unquestionable papal infallibility. Following this, he was able to control the finances of the Catholic Church and the Vatican City to his own advantage, placing himself and his church well beyond the reach of the law or any taxes and enabling money to be invested in shady, underhand schemes around the world. The conservative elements of the church were delighted, but the more liberal factions were horrified with the situation.

The conservatives and reformers reached an impasse during the reign of several popes, with some considering a reform of the Vatican's hierarchy and others desperate to hold on to what they saw as the glory days of total papal freedom created by his untouchable status.

Pope John Paul I's modest and self-effacing demeanour appealed to the conservatives, who saw him as a perfect candidate whom they could effectively control. And yet, once elected in August 1978, the new pope began to display a charisma that had been hidden by his former reserve. He devoted himself entirely to revolutionizing the papacy and to returning it to its spiritual origins. He refused to be sucked into the empty ritual of his predecessors and would not follow the scripts prepared for him by the conservatives at his press conferences. The conservative factions began to despair, especially after he began to express positive views on contraception.

The final straw came when the newly elected pope started to delve into the Vatican Bank's dealings. Uncovering a whole network of corruption involving the Mafia, bribery and extortion, Pope John Paul called Cardinal Villot, the leader of the powerful, conservative Curia, to his study to discuss certain changes that he intended to put into action. Several people were going to be forced to "resign" and among these were the head of the Vatican Bank and several members of the Curia, including Villot himself. Moreover, Villot was told, the Pope would also call a meeting with a US delegation to discuss a reconsideration of the Church's position on birth control.

By the time the Pope retired for the night on the evening of 28 September 1978, taking with him the paperwork that would reveal the Vatican's dealings with the Mafia, he had made himself more enemies than ever. And when his housekeeper tried to rouse him early the next morning, there was no response. Returning a while later, she found the Pope sitting in bed with an awful grimace on his face, the papers still in his hand. Beside him lay a bottle of pills for his blood pressure and he had been sick. Her first port of call was Villot. Villot summoned the doctor immediately. Having done so, he made haste to the Pope's rooms and gathered the bottle of pills along with the precious papers. That was the last that was seen of these items.

To add to these suspicious circumstances, there are other theories concerning the Pope's death. One is that the Vatican Bank, having had shares in the collapsed Banco Ambrosiano, had lost up to a quarter of a billion dollars in the incident and had become involved with the dubious underground Masonic lodge Propaganda Due. P2, as they were known, had connections with the collapsed bank and had been involved in the highly suspect channelling of funds from the US to several groups they supported around the world. Since they were an extremely conservative group and presumably did not want the Pope discovering further illicit dealings between them and the Vatican Bank, P2 had good reason for wanting to remove the Pope to bring an end to his investigations and curb his liberal reign.

There is still no public death certificate for this Pope. Although Italian law requires a period of at least 24 hours before a body may be embalmed, Villot made sure that Pope John Paul I's body was embalmed within 12 hours. And while the convention for embalming dictates that the blood and internal organs be removed, the Pope's corpse was left as it was, hence no one was able to verify whether he had been poisoned or not.

POPE JOHN PAUL II

On 13 May 1981, Pope John Paul II was shot and very nearly killed in St Peter's Square. It was accepted by many that this was the action of an individual madman called Mehmet Ali Ağca. Even at the time, Italian authorities suggested that this might be a part of a larger conspiracy, but this was largely ignored. The Western press suggested that Ağca may in fact have been a cog in the wheel of a Turkish right-wing Islamic fundamentalist conspiracy, but this was as far as it went.

The finger has also been pointed at the Soviet KGB, operating through the secret factions of the communist regimes in Bulgaria and the Turkish Mafia. Rumour has it that Ağca escaped from a Turkish prison and, having been given extensive training and an elaborate plot, adopted a right-wing disguise to hide the real motivations of the assassination.

The plot to kill the Pope may have failed, but this may not have been the sole purpose of the assassination attempt. The whole thing could have been a clever double bluff. After all, what better way to stir up public reaction against right-wing extremity and religious "fundamentalism"? No one suspected the communist role for a minute.

This does raise some doubts as to whether the neo-Nazi activities that have plagued Germany for more than half a century are propagated by extreme right-wing factions at all, or whether the communists are also behind the series of events which have included the branding of the swastika, militant homophobia and racial prejudice, as some doubters believe. Information leaked from within the Soviet Party revealed that one of its primary aims was to stir up public emotion against all that it termed as right-wing. Hitler sympathizers were one obvious example, but other right-wing factions included Christians, Liberals – in fact, anyone who was not communist.

THE PORT CHICAGO DISASTER

In 1944 the Port Chicago disaster killed hundreds of US Navy servicemen in a matter of seconds. On the night of 17 July, two ships loading ammunition in the port's naval base were destroyed in a gigantic explosion. The loading pier and the two ships were decimated and the nearby town of Port Chicago was also badly damaged. Over 300 US sailors were killed outright and several hundred were maimed.

Officially, the world's first nuclear test took place at Alamogordo in New Mexico, but speculation has arisen as to whether the Port Chicago blast may in fact have been an atomic experiment. It was at this time that specifications for the U-235 bomb used at Hiroshima were completed. Hardware for at least three bombs had been ordered by the end of March 1944, and by the previous December 74 kilograms of uranium was available. The US government claimed that the explosion could not have been caused by a bomb as there was not enough uranium available for construction, but based on the above evidence, this would appear to be a lie. In fact, 15.5 kilograms of uranium is all that is needed to build an atomic bomb. If a nuclear weapon was tested at Port Chicago, it is likely to have been one of those built after March 1944.

The total disintegration of the ships and the widespread destruction would suggest that the force of the blast was far greater than even hundreds of tons of high explosives could have caused. Witnesses told of a blinding white flash, which is now known to be characteristic of nuclear explosions, reaching millions of degrees Celsius in millionths of a second. Moreover, the typical nuclear fireball and condensation cloud also point to atomic testing.

The Los Alamos National Laboratory team studied the Port Chicago incident and found that the resulting damage was in keeping with what would have been expected from a relatively small nuclear explosion. A photo technician on the team named Paul Masters kept copies of some of the study documents at his home. In 1980 Peter Vogel found one of them in a yard sale that contained the line: *Ball of fire mushroom out at 18,000 ft in typical Port Chicago fashion*. This was the starting point for Vogel's investigation into the possibility that the Port Chicago explosion was caused by a nuclear bomb, a theory which provoked much controversy. His theories and two decades' worth of clues are summarized in his online book, *The Last Wave from Port Chicago*.

PREDICTIVE PROGRAMMING

The predictive programming theory, which is voiced by many proponents, particularly among alternative media researchers, suggests that public media are deliberately seeded with clues about future changes, be they social, political or technological. All visual media – including the news, television programmes and films – are part of the conspiracy. The concept is that, having been exposed to ideas through visual media, when the changes are later introduced, the public will passively accept them rather than offering resistance. Essentially, it is thought to be a means of subliminal propaganda, or even mass psychological conditioning.

One example often cited is *The Hunger Games: Catching Fire* by Suzanne Collins, for the totalitarian government it depicts. According to the theory, such a government would be more likely to be accepted after people had read this book or watched this film. The fact that the government in the story are seen as the enemy does not come into it – simple exposure will lead to acceptance.

Part of the reasoning behind this is that, having been seen in a surrealist way – particularly through science fiction or fantasy films – if something were to happen in the real world, it would take on that same edge of not being quite real and therefore people would be less likely to fight against it.

Perhaps it is time to turn off those television sets then, or maybe the next thing we see will come to be...

THE PROTOCOLS OF THE ELDERS OF ZION

The Protocols of the Elders of Zion is a document that has been branded, increasingly flimsily, since the end of the nineteenth century as evidence of Jewish plans to take over the world. *The Protocols* are claimed to be the minutes of a meeting of Jewish leaders at the inaugural Zionist Congress in Basel, Switzerland, in 1897.

This manifesto of manipulation and oppression is alleged to include instructions on how finance, war and religion can be used as instruments of control, as well as on brainwashing, suppression, the abuse of authority and the arrest of opponents. *The Protocols* are presented by some as evidence of a Jewish plot to rule the world as an autocracy.

However, the authenticity of *The Protocols* is fiercely contested. Many believe it is an anti-Semitic fake plagiarized from a mid-nineteenth-century Machiavellian satire about the imperialist ambitions of Napoleon III. According to this theory, the name of the first president of the French republic was simply replaced with the word "Judaism".

The first appearance of the papers is dated back to early-twentieth-century Russia, where it was published over the next decade or so in various formats. This research links its emergence to a growing belief that Jews lay behind the country's domestic and foreign woes, in particular the loss of the Russo–Japanese War in 1905.

That English language versions of *The Protocols* should arrive and be published with increased frequency in the US and Europe in the 1920s and 1930s helps support the idea that the document was a racist hoax. With Europe struggling to recover from World War One, economies on both sides of the Atlantic were sliding toward depression, and the blame for this was laid by some at the feet of the Jewish population.

Were *The Protocols* an opportunity for the disenfranchised masses to vent their anger and frustration? Tellingly, the document was used by Hitler and subsequently his Nazi party as justification of the persecution of Jews, initially in Germany and then eventually across Europe.

The discovery of the basic tenets of the supposed *Protocols* in documents relating to alleged subversive plots by the Illuminati, the Freemasons and even aliens casts yet further doubt over their validity. Nevertheless, some still believe that *The Protocols of the Elders of Zion* are a blueprint for Jewish world domination.

QUEEN ELIZABETH I

No definitive reasons have surfaced as to why Elizabeth I never married; certainly an air of ambiguity seems to lie over that part of her life. Not only would this state of affairs have been perceived as undesirable, but it was quite unthinkable not to provide an immediate heir to the throne. There has been speculation that the Queen was malformed and that her inability to produce children was only one manifestation of her dysfunctional sexuality.

This has been taken one step further by some historians who claim that Elizabeth I was in fact a man. There is no doubt that her disguise was artful if this was indeed the case, and it would provide one answer as to why she never married. The theory runs that at the tender age of three, the infant Queen went to stay with some distant cousins. Falling ill while she was there, they could not save her and she died. Terrified of incurring the wrath of her father, Henry VIII, who would have beheaded them without hesitation, the family dressed up a little boy to take her place. This charade continued, apparently, until her death and would explain why she was bald and remained celibate.

RENNES-LE-CHÂTEAU

The appearance of the book *The Holy Blood and the Holy Grail* written by Michael Baigent, Henry Lincoln and Richard Leigh in 1982, sparked waves of controversy throughout the Western world. Lincoln's discovery of the unsolved mysteries shrouding the tiny French hamlet of Rennes-le-Château unveiled a conspiracy spiralling back to the birth of Christ. Could new light be thrown on the last 2,000 years of our history?

The first mystery surrounds the parish priest in the village at the end of the nineteenth century. His name was Bérenger Saunière. Between 1885–1891 his salary averaged very much what one would expect from a rural curate at the time and he led a quiet, simple life. For a long time he had wanted to restore the village church, which stood on the foundations of a much older structure dating back to the sixth century. It was in a state of almost hopeless disrepair. Funded modestly by the village, Saunière embarked upon a plan of restoration, finding inside one of the hollow altar columns four parchments preserved in sealed wooden tubes. The parchments consisted of a series of seemingly incomprehensible codes, but with time their messages became clearer. The raised letters in the second parchment spelled out a coherent message: *To Dragobert II and to Sion belongs this treasure and he is there dead.* Although unsure as to its meaning, Saunière realized that he had stumbled across something of importance and immediately went to Paris in the hope of finding answers. Saunière spent three weeks there. What happened is unknown, but we do know that he, a provincial country priest, was welcomed into the most distinguished ecclesiastical circles.

It was after this trip that the mystery started to thicken. Lincoln shows that, for a start, Saunière's expenditure seemed to go far beyond his means. By the end of his life in 1917, it is calculated that he had spent millions of francs, often in seemingly bizarre ways. The church was redecorated, but redecorated in the most unconventional way, so that above the doorway, a Latin inscription bore the message *Terribilis est locus iste* (This place is terrible), and the garish frescoes on the church walls all seemed to deviate from biblical teaching. In the Ninth Station of the Cross, for example, which shows Jesus' body being carried into the tomb, there is a background of a full moon. What message was being put across here? The Bible would have it that Jesus' burial occurred during the afternoon, so is this simply an interpretation that the burial actually happened at nightfall? Or is it a representation of the body being carried into the tomb at all? Could it be in fact the depiction of Jesus being carried out of, rather than into, the tomb?

Saunière's life became more and more mysterious. His entry into the upper ranks of Parisian society seemed incongruous to say the least, but this did not pose as many questions as the Church's intense interest in his findings, or his subsequent exemption from the Vatican. Rumour has it that on being called to give last rites to Saunière, the neighbouring parish priest fled from Saunière's sickroom, visibly distraught, and refused to perform the ceremony. According to one witness he never smiled again. And why should Saunière's housekeeper, Marie Dénarnaud, who became his lifetime companion, have referred to a "secret" that would give her not only wealth but also power?

It could have been that Saunière had stumbled across a huge sum of money somewhere in the proceedings. But Lincoln explores the possibility that he had discovered something far more incendiary, indeed dangerous. Could it be that he had come across knowledge that would affect the entire Western vision of religious history? Could his money have been part of a vast ecclesiastical blackmailing scheme? Or even a payment for silence? Whatever the answer, the Vatican appeared to be afraid of him throughout his lifetime, and waited on his every command. Whether he was blackmailing them we do not know, but he did appear to have an influence which extended far beyond the provincial backwater of Rennes-le-Château. On his deathbed he passed the secret to his housekeeper. She took the secret to her grave. The mystery continues.

Lincoln says himself that he never set out to discredit the tenets of Christianity, but his research, inspired by the mystery surrounding Saunière, points to a network of conspiracy and obscurity which cannot help but throw the entire Christian culture into question. His hypothesis revolves around the idea that Jesus was in fact married. There is no explicit statement in the Gospels to support this, but if Jesus was claiming the status of rabbi, this would almost be a prerequisite. Jewish law stated quite categorically that an unmarried man may not be a teacher. Moreover, the account of the Wedding at Cana raises questions as to whether this ceremony was in fact Jesus' own wedding – with the presence of Mary, the mother of Jesus, and the repeated references to the bridegroom, addressed to Jesus. One could conclude that Jesus and the bridegroom are one and the same.

Lincoln goes on to show how, if Jesus was married, biblical evidence would appear to point to his wife being either Mary Magdalene, whose role throughout the Gospels seems deliberately ambiguous, or Mary of Bethany. There is also the suggestion that the two Marys were actually the same person. As Lincoln points out, the medieval Church and popular tradition definitely regarded them as such. One woman, recurring throughout the Gospels under different names and performing different roles, could have been the wife of Jesus.

And if Jesus was married, could this have been a marriage to establish a dynasty, a bloodline that would have threatened the entire Roman order?

The question of whether Jesus did father children is, again, far from explicit in the Gospels, but, following Lincoln's argument, one can question the status of Barabbas. If Jesus had had a son, it is indeed likely that he would be called "Jesus bar rabbi", "Jesus, son of the rabbi". Alternatively, "Jesus bar Abba", "Jesus the son of the father" might again refer to Jesus' son, if he were indeed the Heavenly Father.

And the whole issue of the crucifixion is again fraught with ambiguity, as Lincoln shows. Crucifixion was a Roman practice and was reserved exclusively for those who had committed crimes against the empire. This would suggest that Jesus must have done something to provoke the wrath of the

Roman Empire, rather than Jewish law. Moreover, victims of crucifixion usually took over a week to die, yet Jesus' death seems to have been well timed to fit in with Old Testament prophecy. And according to Roman law, a crucified man was denied burial, being simply left on the cross to rot.

If Jesus did not die on the cross, what happened to him and where did he go? Did the resurrection ever actually take place, or was this all part of the grand escape on the part of Jesus? According to certain Eastern legends, he lived until he was well into his 70s, and, Lincoln argues, the documents found by Saunière at Rennes-le-Château contained "incontrovertible proof" that Jesus was still alive in 45 CE.

Quite apart from what happened to him, what happened to his family? If Jesus was indeed married with children, escape would have been as imperative for them as it was for him. Lincoln goes on to ask whether they could have escaped into the south of France. Could Jesus' mummified body even be somewhere near Rennes-le-Château? And could they have brought the dynasty of Jesus into France? Was Jesus' familial genealogy in fact no more miraculous than any of the rest of us? Obviously, we cannot point to any one individual as a direct descendant of Jesus, but if this is the case, it would seem that the entire values and thinking of the Western world would be severely challenged.

Saunière's secret was well kept. But did he unearth a huge cover-up on the part of the Church, obscured by legend and lost in time? One can see why the Church at the end of the nineteenth century was so anxious that he should not speak out.

THE REPTILIAN ELITE

There are many theories surrounding the rich and powerful. The British royal family, the president of the US, heads of large global corporations – all often come under scrutiny. However, one theory does concern everyone in power – the reptilian elite.

According to this theory, all those in positions of power are actually shape-shifting, reptilian humanoids who aim to enslave humanity. Anyone who holds sway could be part of the reptilian elite – actors, musicians, politicians... They exist only to control the population. They are, according to some, responsible for all disasters, including 9/11, the Oklahoma City bombing and even the Holocaust. Former BBC reporter David Icke has been a vocal proponent of this theory, and published a book called *The Biggest Secret* in 1999, which claims, among other things, that the royal family are reptiles. Icke continues to be popular among theorists, running his own alternative news website, and in 2010 released a book explaining how everything is, in fact, being run from the moon.

CONSPIRACY THEORIES

The reptile theory still proves to be a powerful draw to some. If theorists are right, these creatures could be anyone, and will eat you if you get in their way – what a perfect way to dispose of the evidence!

ROBERT MAXWELL

The web of intrigue that surrounded Robert Maxwell throughout his life only began to unravel after his death in November 1991. While soaking up the sun aboard his yacht off the Canary Islands, he mysteriously vanished overboard, just as revelations about his dubious financial dealings began to emerge.

The former Mirror Group chairman and pensions thief was allegedly involved in a $40 billion money-laundering operation with the Russian Mafia and a group of Chinese Triads. He was also close to conspirators in the coup against Russian President Mikhail Gorbachev in 1991, and was on the periphery of the Iran–Contra affair. At the same time, he moved with ease among the world's power brokers and had access to the most secretive places in the world, including the Oval Office and the Kremlin. Given his controversial and dangerous background, it is hardly surprising that his death, to this day, is shrouded in mystery.

Numerous conspiracy theories exist about Maxwell's "assassination", many of which tend to mix the fanciful with the factual. The most popular school of thought claims that he died due to his close association with Mossad, the Israeli Secret Service. It is alleged that Mossad agents chose to eliminate Maxwell because he was threatening to expose Israeli state secrets. Indeed, the death has all the hallmarks of a Mossad operation. According to supporters of the Mossad theory, Israeli agents boarded Maxwell's yacht, the *Lady Ghislaine*, under cover of darkness and plunged a needle filled with a lethal nerve serum into his neck. They then lowered his body into the sea to make his death seem like a suicide.

As well as having close ties with Israel, Maxwell is said to have been a conduit for the Communist Secret Service (SB), setting up countless companies on behalf of former members of the KGB, East German Stasi and Bulgarian government. It is also suspected that Eastern European crime bosses and governments swallowed up billions of Maxwell's laundered money after his death.

ROSWELL

What really happened at Roswell? No other UFO incident has attracted as much attention as the event here in 1947. The theory is that at least one, possibly two, flying saucers crashed in New Mexico during July of that year and that a rancher named Mac Brazel found some of the debris from the crash. The alleged alien wreckage and the bodies of its supposed inhabitants were retrieved immediately and taken away for further investigation. No one knows what happened to them and no one seemed very keen to divulge any information, suggesting that whatever had been discovered was quite possibly of enormous danger to our civilization.

The whole case lay forgotten until 1978, when Stanton Friedman and William L. Moore rediscovered the Roswell reports and pieced together evidence that Brazel had indeed found parts of an alien spacecraft. They worked out a flight path for the UFO: according to them, it came from somewhere south-east of Roswell, suffered some kind of damage or accident over Brazel's ranch where it shed some debris, then veered west to crash in the desert in the region of St Augustine. It was made very clear to them, however, that the US authorities would be no more forthcoming than they had been 30 years before. And it was not just the government who seemed determined to keep something secret. When Lydia Sleppy, a teletype operator in Albuquerque, was putting reports of the crashed saucer on to the air, her machine ground to a halt. Then, says *The Roswell Incident* by Berlitz and Moore, it came out with this curt message: *ATTENTION ALBUQUERQUE: DO NOT TRANSMIT. REPEAT DO NOT TRANSMIT THIS MESSAGE. STOP COMMUNICATION IMMEDIATELY.* The sender was not identified.

Someone does not want the truth of the incident to be revealed. And so, we can ask, was the crashed object really an alien craft? Or could there be a very dark and dreadful secret behind what really went on?

Of course, the object could have been a balloon, either a weather balloon or the test launch of a balloon in the top-secret Project Mogul. According to surviving project members of Mogul, a large number of these balloons could certainly have crashed on to Brazel's ranch, and their remains would fit his description of what he found. Mogul's classified purpose was to try and develop a way to monitor possible Soviet nuclear waves and no other means of investigating the nuclear activities of a closed country like the USSR were available yet. The project was given a high priority. And yet the whole Roswell mystery could be no more than a military failure to tell a balloon from an alien flying saucer.

However, there are more unnerving possibilities. Suppose the balloon was the top-secret device which was going to win the Cold War for the US? Suppose it crashed on its first flight and that a serious investigation would have revealed that it was hopeless and only carried out because of a network of corrupt government contracts and dealings? Or perhaps there is a still murkier Roswell secret, such as the possibility that it could have been a tethered balloon carrying a nuclear device designed to explode at high altitude? Suppose it had broken free, depositing its lethal cargo near Roswell, with the town avoiding complete destruction by only a tiny margin? This would be the kind of event that officials would go to any lengths to hide, even by creating elaborate UFO contact stories once the investigations started.

In 1948, a year after the incident, Bernard Newman, a British writer, produced a book whose theme was uncomfortably close to the events at Roswell. It told of a faked UFO crash orchestrated by leading world scientists whose aim was to force world disarmament. If this was in fact the case, it would suggest that what happened at Roswell may have carried a political agenda, or even that the incident was spelling out some kind of warning.

RUDOLF HESS

One of the enduring mysteries of World War Two is the nature of the role played by Rudolf Hess in the hostilities and what became of him. Hess was deputy to the Führer and first in line to succeed Adolf Hitler, should he be eliminated. In 1941, on the eve of war with the Soviet Union, Hess flew over Britain, unarmed, and landed in Scotland. His aim was to negotiate a peace deal with Britain, but instead he was promptly arrested. The official story goes that he was then tried at Nuremberg and sentenced to life behind bars at Spandau Prison, Berlin, where he died in 1987. His one-man mission would appear to be the work of a lunatic, but conspiracy theorists have been loath to accept that he acted alone, and question the fact that he was left imprisoned in Spandau long after other convicts were released.

One theory goes that he actually arrived in Scotland with the full knowledge and support of Hitler, acting as his personal envoy. It is argued that he was to meet a member of the royal family to organize a peace treaty between Britain and Germany. Hitler was thought to want to avoid conflict with Britain if he could because he understood how difficult it would be to conquer the island, with simultaneous eastern and western fronts an enormous drain on his military arsenal, settling for continental Europe as the limit of his imperialist ambitions.

When Winston Churchill was notified of this plan, however, he was determined to prevent its fruition. Churchill had been an impassioned critic of Hitler, and his disgust of the German appeasers within Britain had encouraged his belligerence toward Nazi Germany, which he viewed as a scourge on the face of Europe – one that he was determined to defeat. He instructed the army to imprison Hess as soon as he arrived on British soil.

In a further twist, it is claimed that Hess used an anonymous double. While the fake Hess was kept in a Welsh prison, the real one was still in Scotland. This prevented any rescue attempts on him by German special forces. In an attempt to undermine Churchill, the Duke of Kent – part of the establishment keen on a peace deal with Hitler – flew to Iceland. On his journey he stopped off in Scotland to collect the real Hess and take him to Sweden to initiate a peace plan. Intriguingly, the plane crashed on leaving Scotland and those on board were killed instantly.

But why would the aristocracy have become involved in such a scheme? They viewed the Nazi threat as much less important than the threat from the Soviet Union. They thought that if they could enable Hitler to concentrate all his efforts on the Eastern Front he would have greater success in defeating Stalin's empire. This would leave both the Soviets and the Germans severely weakened, with a power and territorial vacuum in Western Europe ready to be exploited by the British.

With the Duke of Kent's plan foiled, it was simply left for the fake Hess to take the stand at the Nuremberg trials, where

Hermann Goering claimed: "Hess? Which Hess? The Hess you have here? Our Hess? Your Hess?" If this elaborate plan and counter-plan were true, it certainly might have been possible to conceal them amid the euphoria of the Allies' victory, when people preferred to look forward to a more optimistic future.

In November 2003, a programme called *The Queen's Lost Uncle* was broadcast on British television. In it, claims were made that unspecified "recently released" documents had revealed that Hess flew to the UK to meet Prince George, Duke of Kent, but the Prince was rushed away from the scene when Hess' arrival was botched. According to this theory, the Prince was acting as part of a plot to trick the Nazis into believing that he and other senior figures were conspiring to overthrow Winston Churchill.

Although it is recorded that Hess eventually committed suicide in prison, his lawyer, Alfred Seidl, claimed that Hess was actually murdered. He alleged that two MI6 agents were sent to kill the imprisoned German amid fears that he might be released by the newly tolerant Soviet leadership and spill his secrets about the secret peace negotiations Churchill tried to carry out, which were contrary to the British leader's assertion that he would only allow peace when the Nazis had surrendered. Seidl points to Hess' physical condition at the time; he is supposed to have strangled himself with electrical cord, but Hess was suffering from terrible arthritis and couldn't even perform simple actions, such as tying his laces, without help. It follows, Seidl claims, that he would have been physically unable to carry out the actions needed to kill himself. Seidl also highlighted that the autopsy report carried out by a British Army doctor was inaccurate and is evidence that the British military were trying to cover up Hess' murder.

A second autopsy, performed by a German pathologist, suggested that the marks on Hess' neck were not consistent with suicide, although the report could not find any evidence of a third party's involvement in the death.

RUSSIAN APARTMENT BOMBINGS

Between 4–16 September 1999, five bombs exploded in four apartment buildings in Moscow, Buynaksk and Volgodonsk, claiming nearly 300 lives and injuring hundreds more. The series of attacks spread fear across Russia, and has been the subject of controversy ever since.

The Russian government, led by President Boris Yeltsin and Prime Minister Vladimir Putin, were quick to point the finger of blame at Chechen rebels, who were accused of mounting the attacks in retaliation to state defiance of their efforts to establish independence, but others would argue that the state itself was not beyond suspicion.

Many believe that the bombings were orchestrated by the FSB, the Russian Secret Service (and successor to the KGB), in order to increase public support for the second Chechen war, which had begun in August, and to expedite the rise of their former boss, Vladimir Putin, to the presidency.

Dubbed Operation Successor, this alleged *coup d'état* was successful. After Yeltsin's surprise early retirement at the end of 1999, Putin took the highest office in Russia less than a year after the bombings, cruising to victory on a wave of popularity which was engendered in part thanks to the acceleration of direct action in Chechnya and a call for renewed national solidarity.

This theory has been backed by a number of anti-Kremlin oligarchs and political refugees, including exiled billionaire businessman Boris Berezovsky and ex-FSB officer Alexander Litvinenko, who published his beliefs in the book *Blowing Up Russia: The Secret Plot to Bring Back KGB Terror.*

Evidence was produced that showed that an FSB agent was renting the basement of one of the apartment buildings attacked, while theorists also point to the government's sudden U-turn over the use of the military explosive RDX as further indication of government involvement. The state initially claimed that RDX was used to make the bombs, but after it was discovered that the substance could only be sourced from a heavily protected state site, they changed their story and denied it had been found.

Furthermore, an attempted bombing of an apartment block in Ryazan, just days after the last attack in Volgodonsk, was traced back to FSB agents. After initial denials, the head of the FSB apologized and admitted his organization's activity, claiming that those involved were carrying out an untimely training exercise.

Yuri Shchekochikhin and Sergei Yushenkov, two prominent members of an independent body commissioned to investigate the role of the FSB in the attacks, both met mysterious deaths in 2003, while journalist Anna Politkovskaya was murdered in October 2006 when following a similar line of inquiry. Litvinenko died in mysterious circumstances in London later the same year.

However, the finger of blame was thrust not only at the Russian government. Warlord Al-Khattab, who had links with the terrorist groups Liberation Army of Dagestan and the Islamic Army of Dagestan, was considered the culprit by some. He was said to have launched the attacks in response to Russian military aggression in and around Dagestan and Chechnya prior to the bombings.

Others claim that the anti-consumerist Revolutionary Writers' group was to blame. A note from the organization was allegedly discovered by the FSB in the rubble of one of the bombed-out apartment blocks admitting the act, carried out in protest at the rapid spread of capitalist-fuelled consumerism across the formerly communist country.

SARS VIRUS

The Severe Acute Respiratory Syndrome (SARS) virus hit the headlines in late 2002, quickly spreading panic across the world. The outbreak lasted until the summer of 2003. Over 8,000 cases and almost 800 deaths were reported. But was SARS a naturally occurring pandemic or something more sinister?

There are those who believe that SARS was a man-made virus, pointing to claims made by two prominent Russian scientists in the midst of the outbreak. Nikolai Filatov, chief of epidemiological services in Moscow, and Sergei Kolesnikov, a member of Russia's Academy of Medical Sciences, publicly stated that the virus was a cocktail of mumps and measles which could not have formed naturally.

If these claims were true, for what purpose was SARS created? Some believe that it was created in US government laboratories as a biological weapon to destabilize one of its fiercest enemies. Haven't events of recent years shown the detrimental impact on US trade and its general fiscal health of the rapid development of the Chinese economy? Isn't it convenient that the World Health Organization (WHO) reported just 27 cases of SARS and no fatalities in the US, whereas by far the most reported cases and deaths relating to SARS were in China?

Theorists believe that the US government was able to create a virus whose potency was tailored to the Chinese race by using blood samples collected by US medical and pharmaceutical joint ventures in China. Others go on to claim that the Japanese colluded in this plot to engineer a deadly disease, supplying blood samples from its factories in China.

Other theorists point the finger at the Chinese state. They believe that SARS was a biological weapon developed by Chinese government scientists and that the pandemic occurred because of some kind of accident at the laboratories where it was being manufactured and stored. This theory would explain the high levels of domestic exposure, and the government's initial attempts to cover up the severity of the outbreak and their reluctance to cooperate with the WHO.

Another theory suggests that SARS was developed by a shadowy group of industrialists and politicians, known as the New World Order, as a tool to effect population control. The world's population is becoming unmanageable and the drain on natural resources is at a critical level. This group apparently believes that the answer to these problems lies in reducing the number of people on the planet by at least a third. Was SARS just an experiment in assembling the perfect biological weapon capable of wiping out the lives of over two billion people?

SPACE SHUTTLE *COLUMBIA*

When the NASA space shuttle *Columbia* exploded upon re-entry to Earth's orbit on 1 February 2003 following a successful space mission, was it a mere accident or the result of something far more disquieting?

Despite the crash taking place in Texas, the main focus of curiosity centred on a potential link to the Arab–Israeli conflict in the Middle East. The vapour trails from the disintegrating aircraft were first seen over the town of Palestine, Texas, which is also where the first debris was found. One of the six crew members on board was Colonel Ilan Ramon, Israel's first-ever astronaut. Ramon was a former Israeli Air Force pilot, who participated in the bombing of Iraq's Osirak nuclear reactor in 1981. The crash took place against the backdrop of the military build-up of US and coalition forces in anticipation of the Iraq War, and increasing hostility in the Middle East to the US and the perceived enemies of the Arab world, primarily Israel. With fierce Arab condemnation of Israel's occupation of the West Bank and, as they see it, the brutal persecution of the Palestinian people, the irony of the crash location, Palestine, Texas, seems too much of a coincidence for some.

For those who like to create or uncover anti-Zionist conspiracies, these facts seem to point to only one thing: divine intervention. Palestinian terrorist organizations described it as "punishment from Allah". Many of those who believe in a connection are active Holocaust-deniers, and they seized on the fact that Colonel Ramon's parents were both Holocaust survivors, and that Ramon took on board with him Holocaust-related items and literature.

Apocryphal stories also emerged suggesting Colonel Ramon was conducting secret experiments on the shuttle mission on behalf of Israel's Institute of Biological Research, looking at ways of combating the potential threat of Saddam Hussein's weapons of mass destruction. It was alleged that Ramon was using covert cameras to survey desert dust and wind drifts emanating from Iraq's deserts, providing intelligence which would assist in repelling possible future attacks.

Others point to the US government and believe it is a self-inflicted disaster, a "textbook psychological warfare operation", designed to create public anger against Iraq and the wider Arab world to prepare people psychologically to support the Iraq War. Even without explicit confirmation from the government, the tacit link would be enough to increase support for a controversial conflict. A similar plan to this was developed in the 1960s, code-named Operation Northwoods. It was drawn up by the Joint Chiefs of Staff and aimed to blame Cuba if anything went wrong during the mission to launch John Glenn as the first US citizen to orbit Earth in 1962.

THE SPHINX AND THE GREAT PYRAMID

The ancient Egyptians built their monuments on a scale which continues to impress even modern scholars and tourists. The grandest of their monuments, and possibly the most debated, are the Great Pyramid and the Sphinx at Giza. These structures, built wholly of solid stone blocks weighing 200 tons each, have fascinated visitors since their construction, the techniques of which have been lost to history.

Could the Egyptian kings, scheming to create a lasting and powerful display of Egyptian ingenuity, have created the structures for the express purpose of confusing future civilizations as to just exactly how they were built? With theories of vast slave pools, unknown ancient technology and even alien assistance, the mystery of the pyramids will likely live on far into human history.

Another theory suggests that perhaps the monuments were not built by the Egyptians at all. The Great Sphinx of Giza is not built out of quarried rock like the pyramids and temples that it guards, but rather out of the unbroken foundation. It has a man's (or arguably a woman's) head and the body of a lion. It is 20 metres high, 73 metres long and has the most extraordinary expression, looking out of this world into infinity. Most Egyptologists, and most Egyptians for that matter, believe that the Sphinx was built around 2500 BCE during the rule of Pharaoh Chephren, who was also responsible for the construction of the second pyramid at Giza. Recent research has shown that this theory is little more than legend, but this is a theory well worth upholding on the Egyptians' part, for the monumental edifice has become a symbol of their kingdom.

John A. West, a renowned Egyptologist, has visited the statue many times and it had always seemed to him to be something apart, something far older than known civilization. While reading a book on Egypt by the French author and mathematician Schwaller de Lubicz, he came across the theory that there were signs of water erosion on the body of the Sphinx. West realized that the weathering patterns on the Sphinx were not horizontal, as seen on other monuments at Giza, but vertical. Horizontal weathering is the result of prolonged exposure to strong winds and sandstorms. There have been plenty of these in the arid area of the Sahara, but could water have caused the vertical weathering on the Sphinx? Water from where?

In 1991 Dr Robert Schoch, a prominent geologist and professor at Boston University, examined the weathering on the Sphinx and concluded in his findings that the patterns must have been caused by torrential rain, which would imply that the Sphinx had been built in an era when such rains were common in the area and that the other monuments must have been erected many years later. This would suggest that the

THE SPHINX AND THE GREAT PYRAMID

Sphinx was built before the most ancient of Egyptians, before the very first dynasties thousands of years before Christ – before, in fact, recorded history. And this would give weight to some staggering possibilities.

The Sphinx is quite possibly the most remarkable monument in the world. It is unlike anything either the ancient Egyptians or even our modern culture could construct. It seems to belong to an ancient culture, and one which must have had far greater technical know-how than ours. Its face is surprisingly modern and its expression is one of such wisdom and profundity that it suggests knowledge far beyond our limited intelligence. We can only speculate as to the secrets the Sphinx guards, but whatever they are the Egyptians do not want them to be revealed.

The pharaonic head of the Sphinx is out of proportion with the body. Could it have originally been a leonine head, carved 12,000 years ago to mark the Age of Leo, which was rediscovered just 4,000 years ago by the Egyptians and then re-carved at that point in honour of their pharaoh?

A series of surveys has also indicated the existence of several tunnels under the Sphinx itself, leading to an unexplored chamber about 7.5 metres beneath the great paws of the statue. We can only surmise as to what the contents of this chamber might be, but the possibilities are endless. The remnants of an ancient civilization could be stored here. And if this ancient civilization was capable of building the Sphinx, revelations as to its other capabilities could be extremely enlightening. Perhaps therein lies the riddle of the Sphinx.

Moreover, in March 1993, a small door was discovered at the end of a long narrow shaft in the Great Pyramid. Since then, the principal researcher, German Rudolph Gantenbrink, has been forbidden from continuing the exploration. The Egyptian antiquities authorities gave the excuse that, in leaking the news to the British press, Gantenbrink broke a rule of archaeology. Egyptian authorities were adamant that the find was of no importance, but it would appear that they were attempting to hide something.

Other popular theories suggest that the pyramids and the Sphinx were created (or that the Egyptians were assisted in their creation) by superior technology from outer space. On the other hand, in their book *The Stargate Conspiracy*, Lynn Picknett and Clive Prince claim that such theories about alien intervention in the creation of the pyramids are themselves all part of a greater, but less-documented, conspiracy. The bogus idea of extraterrestrial intervention is a deliberate red herring on the part of a much wider conspiracy involving intelligence agencies, whose aim is that people will feel they are subordinate to some form of superior extraterrestrial race. This would create a dependency among humanity upon outside forces and an inferiority complex across the human race. Messages then "intercepted" by governments and intelligence agencies could be used to manipulate a country's population, under the guise of extraterrestrial orders, and to create authoritarian, fascist dictatorships. The world's fascination with ancient Egypt could be the greatest example of this grand scheme.

SUBLIMINAL ADVERTISING

Subliminal advertising is a topic of continual controversy among academics, the advertising industry and big business in general, with the public left in the middle not knowing who to believe or trust. Arguments and insults have been traded repeatedly between scholars and advertisers, with both sides claiming to speak the truth and accusing the other of casting damaging aspersions.

Whenever conspiracy theories are discussed they are often linked to political events, whether by partisan troublemakers or well-intentioned truth seekers. George W. Bush and his party were accused of using subliminal messages during his 2000 election campaign in Florida. In a Republican advert criticizing Democratic candidate Al Gore's prescription drug proposal, the word "RATS" appeared briefly on screen over the words "The Gore Prescription Plan". The letters then formed part of the next message, which read: "Bureaucrats decide".

Owing to the extremely fractious nature of the 2000 election race, and the events in Florida especially, accusing fingers were pointed toward the Bush campaign team. Al Gore claimed,

285

"I've never seen anything like it. I think it speaks for itself." When asked who he thought was behind the "RATS" message, Gore stated: "That's obvious." The advert was shown 4,400 times in 33 television markets across the US.

Subliminal messages often focus on society's taboos. According to Dr Wilson Bryan Key, topics such as sex, death, incest, homosexuality and pagan symbols are all used by advertising companies to get a secret message into a viewer's mind without them realizing it. The advertising agencies claim that any hidden symbols are pure coincidence, a mistake or the result of individual artists going beyond their remit. In his research, however, Key says advertising agencies spend thousands of dollars and hundreds of design hours making sure their adverts are pitched perfectly to their intended target, right down to using death symbols and images of screaming faces, animals and sexual gratification.

With no laws to prevent this kind of activity, there is little to stop advertising agencies resorting to the use of subliminal messages. It is very disturbing indeed to consider the power that advertisers have to conspire to change society's behaviour without our knowledge.

SUGAR

While it is widely accepted that sugar is not great for you and should be consumed in moderation, there are those who believe that sugar is a poison, and that the sugar industry (or "Big Sugar") have been covering up the evidence of its harmful nature for decades, much in the way the tobacco lobbies did with smoking. Indeed, some call for sugar to be regulated, just like alcohol and tobacco.

Up until 1976, advertising suggested that sugar was healthy, that it was good for you. Not only did it give you energy, but it could even help you lose weight! However, these spurious claims were called out by the Federal Trade Commission in the US, and sugar consumption dropped – at least temporarily.

Enter Big Sugar. Theorists believe that money was pumped in by sugar concerns, to make sure that the image of sugar as a safe foodstuff was upheld, despite evidence to the contrary. The claim is that the supposedly independent scientific papers declaring sugar to be safe were skewed, as the funding for said research came from the sugar corporations themselves.

It is hard to ignore the fact that there has been an increase in the amount of sugar eaten in the average Western diet, and that there has been, concurrently, an increase in obesity and weight-related health issues, such as Type 2 diabetes. Some have also linked sugar to heart disease and cancer, though in the US it has GRAS (Generally Regarded As Safe) status, and is used throughout the world.

Others believe that the conspiracy goes deeper. The financial gain of maintaining the "safe" image of sugar is one thing, but imagine a huge group of people addicted to it, continually lining the pockets of Big Sugar. This is the claim – that sugar is, in fact, a drug more than a foodstuff. In the US, sugar is added to around 80 per cent of foods, and highly processed glucose-fructose syrup is often used. It is claimed that this makes sugar inescapable, and that people end up addicted to the pleasure they get from consuming sweetened foods. Sugar does work on the same reward centres in the brain as drugs like cocaine, but as yet there is no definitive evidence that sugar is addictive in the same way. Scientific studies are being carried out, so perhaps this is one conspiracy which will soon come to light.

SWINE FLU

The outbreak of the H1N1 strain of influenza, more commonly known as swine flu, was first reported in Mexico in April 2009. The disease subsequently spread across the world, claiming thousands of lives and reaching official pandemic status as defined by the World Health Organization. But did it occur naturally, as we are led to believe?

One theory is that the virus, composed of an improbable mix of genetic elements from bird flu, swine flu and human flu, was created by a research-based pharmaceutical industry cartel. This group is said to have been under mounting pressure as research pipelines and generic drug competition decimated their profit margins. The H1N1 strain was apparently released in order to generate much-needed revenue.

The likes of GlaxoSmithKline, Roche and Baxter are believed by some to head up this sinister alliance; all three were first on the scene when it came to providing vaccines. The financial gains on offer were truly staggering. Was this not the shot in the arm that these companies had been desperately searching for?

Others believe that al-Qaeda was the perpetrator of a global bioterrorist attack. With security surrounding high-profile countries becoming increasingly hard to break down, the Osama bin Laden-led group chose Mexico for the ease of its accessibility. And, crucially, for its proximity to the US. It is no secret that the Hispanic population in the US is swelling to an unprecedented size and that the flow of immigrants, legal and illegal, from Mexico continues in large numbers. Would Mexicans not represent the ideal vehicle to spread a deadly virus throughout the land of so-called infidels?

Another theory accuses former US president George W. Bush and his industrialist cronies, all reeling from the loss of power, of masterminding the outbreak of the H1N1 influenza strain. These people believe that, without having to coordinate possibly illegal wars in faraway places and unconstitutional domestic reform founded in neo-Conservative and neo-Christian lunacy, and having to witness the cult of Obama, Bush mentally collapsed and launched the outbreak in Mexico as some kind of crazed revenge attack.

Or is it all down to People for the Ethical Treatment of Animals (PETA)? In a desperate attempt to protect the animals of the world and decrease human consumption of meat, this group, or a militant faction within it, could have purposefully spread the likes of mad cow disease, bird flu and swine flu; these diseases have certainly put some people off eating animals.

TITANIC

In 1912 the English cruise liner *Titanic* sank to the bottom of the North Atlantic, taking some two-thirds of its passengers to their icy deaths. The tragedy of the largest liner of its time has long been attributed to a deadly collision with an iceberg by those on board both the ship itself and the rescue vessels.

The ship lay undiscovered for over 70 years until Dr Robert Ballard of the Woods Hole Oceanographic Institute led an expedition which successfully located the sunken shell. Subsequent trips to the wreckage and a more thorough examination of the shattered hull gave rise to a previously unthought-of theory about the ship's demise. Forget the iceberg. The *Titanic* had been sunk by a torpedo.

Supporters of this theory point the finger of blame at the Germans. By 1912 the Germans had perfected the U-boat and built several prototypes for testing. The story goes that the German government distrusted the English, and set to prove them wrong when they proclaimed the ship "unsinkable". The U-boat glided quietly out into the North Atlantic and crept up on the luxury liner. It was simply good fortune and coincidence that the ship happened to pass next to an iceberg – realizing that this would mask their crime, the Germans torpedoed the same side of the ship. The resulting damage sunk the *Titanic* and its passengers. The German U-boat slipped silently away and let the iceberg have the glory.

TRAILER PARKS

On 29 October 1929 the US suffered the worst stock market crash in the nation's history. Suddenly the country plunged from being a fast-growing economic power into a deep and long-lasting crisis of financial loss and chronic unemployment. In 1932 Franklin D. Roosevelt defeated Herbert Hoover in the presidential elections and embarked on the huge social reform intended to rehabilitate the US economy and boost morale among its citizens. His programme ranged from funding for public services to instituting social welfare. The nation's predicament slowly improved and Roosevelt was re-elected a further three times, in 1936, 1940 and 1944 respectively. But was there a darker side to this extensive economic reform that has been kept from the public?

Roosevelt must have known that part of the nation's problem was simply that it was overpopulated. And although a Hitler-esque genocide by the military may have solved the population crisis, that would not do the government's reputation much good. So did he come up with an alternative plan to remove large segments of the country's population without losing face?

CONSPIRACY THEORIES

Theorists suggest that Roosevelt secretly contacted various architects and engineers and instructed them to make, as a priority, the design of a mobile house or "trailer home". These would offer low-income families a home, relative comfort and community life. Land was bought in the Midwestern states and a series of trailer parks was created.

However, the trailer parks were located in a region with an abnormally high incidence of tornadoes. Thus, the plan went, multitudes of tornadoes would hit the trailer parks, eliminating whole families in "natural disasters" for which no individual could be held responsible. Every year, hundreds are injured when tornadoes tear paths of destruction through trailer parks, apparently just as Roosevelt intended.

TUPAC SHAKUR

After leaving the Mike Tyson fight in Las Vegas on Saturday 7 September 1996, Tupac Shakur was allegedly shot five times from a car which had pulled up close to his. He initially survived the shooting and was taken to a nearby hospital. He was pronounced dead on 13 September 1996. That was a Friday the thirteenth. There have been plenty of conspiracy theories relating to the murder, but none has caught on like the notion that Shakur's death is all one big hoax. The theory holds that Shakur wanted to be free of the stifling publicity that went along with his high-profile outlaw lifestyle and that he's now living it up on a desert island somewhere.

Theorists have come up with various bits of "evidence" that support this theory. These include:

- He is seen crucified on the cover of one of his CDs, which would suggest that he will rise again.

- A music video released conveniently just days after his death shows Tupac being murdered, presumably to convince the public that this was what really did happen.

- Tupac always wore a bulletproof vest, no matter where he went. Why didn't he wear it to a very public event like a Tyson fight? Some believe he wanted to make it plausible that a shot would kill him.

- In most of his songs, he talks about being buried, so why was he allegedly cremated the day after he died? Furthermore, it is highly unconventional to cremate someone the day after death without a full investigation. In fact, it is illegal to bury someone who has been murdered if a post-mortem has not been carried out.

- Why couldn't the police locate the white car from which the bullets were fired? After all, Las Vegas is in the middle of the desert, and it would seem really quite improbable that it escaped without being witnessed.

- Tupac's entourage was notorious for having a gangster-like image. So why did none of them shoot back?

An investigation into the killing published in the *Los Angeles Times* concluded that the killer was a man Tupac had been seen attacking earlier in the evening, Orlando Anderson, a member of a rival gang. Anderson was later killed by gunfire in another gangland murder, but until then he had got away with the shooting of Tupac – perhaps he had protection in high places. The most crucial twist in the paper's findings, though, is the supplier of the gun that killed the star: Tupac's main rap-music rival and nemesis, The Notorious B.I.G., who was rumoured to have paid around $1 million for Tupac's demise. Although he denied any involvement, The Notorious B.I.G. was found shot dead in yet another killing just months after Tupac's death, a crime which also remains unsolved. If he was involved, the conspiracy must have been extensive within LA gang culture to provide a cover for him for so long.

THE TURIN SHROUD

The public exhibition of one of the most disputed relics in history has been the subject of much controversy. We know that the large sheet bearing the imprint of a man, known as the Turin Shroud, is believed to be at least several hundred years old and some claim that it dates back as far as 2,000 years. The bearded, long-haired man in the image would seem to have suffered wounds associated with crucifixion and certainly suggests a likeness to Jesus' body. It bears marks along the forehead, which one could presume came from the crown of thorns, flogging wounds and even a cut to the right of his chest. The cloth would appear to be stained with blood.

What rouses the experts' suspicion is how the imprint of the man ever found its way on to the cloth in the first place. It gives an impression similar to a photographic negative, but that would have been quite an achievement 2,000 years ago, or even 1,000 years ago for that matter. One theory goes that Leonardo da Vinci had the technological knowledge to create a photographic image, and that in fact the image on the shroud is a photographic self-portrait of Leonardo himself.

One scientist put forward the theory that the imprint on the shroud is in fact a painting, claiming to find traces of paint on the cloth. However, arguments against this theory suggest that the paint could have rubbed off paintings that the shroud covered in attempts to sanctify them. And others have dismissed this idea by claiming not to have found paintbrush strokes on the shroud.

One piece of evidence pointing to a forgery is that the nail wounds are in the palms of the hands, as was traditionally believed to be the case with Jesus. Historical evidence of crucifixions points to this being a physical impossibility, however: a nail through the palm could not support the body's weight – it would tear through the bones and muscles. Crucifixion was only possible by placing the nail through the wrist, which had a strong enough bone structure. If Jesus' shroud is a fabrication, then it followed tradition rather than scientific fact.

While it may be a clever fake, the origins of the shroud are ambiguous. Even if it had been fabricated in the Middle Ages as the ultimate relic, the precision of the image is astounding. And this cannot explain away the blood stains. One theory would have it that the shroud is not only what it claims to be, but that it is more than this because it is none other than the Holy Grail of myth. Another theorist puts forward the view that the imprinted man is not actually Jesus but one of the Knights Templar, one of the legendary guardians of the Grail.

The Turin Shroud has nearly been the victim of fire three times since its relocation to Turin. On the third occasion, early on 14 April 1997, firemen arrived at the scene to find flames and smoke pouring out of the tops of Turin Cathedral and the neighbouring Guarini Chapel, which was built to house the shroud. Local fireman and hero Mario Trematore used a sledgehammer to break the bulletproof glass which protected the relic and then carried it to safety.

The shroud escaped damage, but the Renaissance cathedral and the chapel, designed by architect Guarino Guarini, suffered extensive damage. The official report points to an electrical fault as the cause of the fire, but an unofficial source has revealed an anti-Catholic conspiracy which targeted the shroud. It is alleged that members of the Southern Baptist Church of North America and extremist fundamentalist factions of the Protestant Church may have set fire to the chapel to destroy the shroud. This would coincide with a new period of attack against Roman Catholicism by reactionary Protestant forces. The destruction of the shroud would certainly have provoked widespread disruption and trauma in the Roman Catholic Church worldwide. The ensuing havoc would have provided rival factions with the perfect opportunity to launch an attack.

The Baptist Church has officially rejected the shroud as a fraud, quoting recent scientific work aimed at dating the linen. However, although the studies indicate that the shroud may have its origins in the Middle Ages, they cannot reach any precise date, nor explain the image for which the shroud is so famous.

UNIFIED CONSPIRACY THEORY

Possibly both the simplest and most complex of all conspiracy theories, the Unified Conspiracy Theory (sometimes referred to as the Grand Unified Conspiracy) tells us that "they" really are out to get you, and "they" are all in on it. In its simplest terms, this theory suggests that absolutely everything is a conspiracy – even other conspiracy theories.

To go into more detail, one facet of this theory is that absolutely all negative things which happen are controlled by a great, evil entity – often believed to be the Illuminati – who creates and manages a huge number of happenings all over the world.

This "super-conspiracy", as Michael Barkun called it, suggests that all conspiracies exist in an interlocking, hierarchical web, subtly controlling the world. If smaller conspiracy theories (those lower down the chain) are proved to be false, the super-conspiracy theory suggests that they are, in fact, all part of the cover-up – trying to keep us from finding out the far greater, large-scale conspiracy truth.

VACCINES AND AUTISM

Scientists have been steadily developing vaccines for ever more diseases over the last 1,000 years to help prevent diseases that once would have proved fatal to thousands every year. Most people accept that childhood vaccinations are a necessary part of growing up, and that if and when they have children, they too will be vaccinated to help them live a longer, healthier life.

There are those, however, who believe that something sinister, a cover-up of huge proportions, lies behind the systematic vaccination of children: vaccines do not work and, in fact, they cause autism in children. The MMR vaccine, which is given to every child in the UK between the ages of 12–15 months, has been blamed particularly strongly. This was backed up by a scientific paper, published in 1998 in *The Lancet* by Andrew Wakefield, but from 2001 onward, and especially in recent years, this has been discredited, with Wakefield himself eventually admitting that it was not based on any solid evidence.

Some others have claimed that the increase in childhood vaccinations is to blame for the increase in childhood illnesses which were hardly seen 20 years ago, such as ADHD. However, the medical world, along with much of the population, seeks to discredit the theorists with the simple fact that diagnostics also developed over that time, and that more children who would have been passed off as simply "difficult" are now getting help for underlying conditions instead.

Of course, many continue to believe that vaccinations could cause serious illness in their children, and still cite Wakefield, the suggestion being that perhaps "Big Pharma" discredited him for fear of losing out on revenue should the dangerous truth about vaccination be uncovered.

VIRTUAL CONSPIRACY

There has been much speculation over a plot to bring Bill Clinton down during his presidency. But if that is the case, then it was no ordinary conspiracy. Unlike the dissidents that met in boarding houses to plot Abraham Lincoln's assassination, this was something of a completely different order, a "virtual" conspiracy.

In a traditional conspiracy, individuals all come together and when they finally move, speed is vitally important. Secrecy is essential. A virtual conspiracy has the same objective of bringing a leader down, but the tactics are different. It starts in the open and requires publicity to grow and gain supporters. By making their moves overtly, they attract others to their cause and to one another.

Freedom of expression is the name of the game here and the virtual conspirators channel their discontent and make false allegations through the press. Whether the allegations succeed or fail, they invariably have some effect, making the target more and more vulnerable.

In this way, the virtual conspirators were unconcerned as to whether the Clintons did or didn't murder Vincent Foster, for example, nor whether the evidence pointed toward Foster having committed suicide. The objective was to get the media to voice the idea of the Clintons as murderers in the hope that someone would come forward with proof. Similarly, it was of little consequence to them whether the Clinton administration did or didn't allocate grave sites at Arlington National Cemetery for political supporters. And the details of the president's various sexual adventures were of no interest whatsoever. Whether Clinton raped a woman in Arkansas when he was attorney general in his home state was neither here nor there. What was important to these virtual conspirators was that these provocative questions wormed their way into the press.

The fantastic thing about being a virtual conspirator is that you can spread the most outrageous rumours about whoever you want and not get personally accused. The reporter you conned may not be best pleased, but the more scandalous the story the better it will sell. An angry denial from the target generates yet more coverage of the actual charge.

THE WACO SIEGE

On 28 February 1993, the US Bureau of Alcohol, Tobacco and Firearms (ATF) attempted to execute a search warrant at the Branch Davidian Ranch at Mount Carmel outside Waco, Texas. Shots were fired and four agents were killed, as well as six followers of David Koresh, the leader of the Davidian group. Over the following 51 days the FBI held the centre under siege. This ended on 19 April, when the FBI mounted an assault and a fire broke out which destroyed the compound, killing 76 people, including Koresh.

So why did the FBI handle the situation in this way? The official line is that toward the end of the siege, agents were concerned that the people inside were about to mount a mass suicide attempt, despite Koresh having made no such suggestion of this during the negotiations. There were also reports of children being abused inside the compound, which increased the pressure to act.

Steve Stockman, a Texan, wrote an article putting forward the conspiracy theory that the Clinton authorities stormed the community in an effort to gain support for gun control.

The Davidian followers inside the ranch were certainly well equipped in the firearms department.

According to Peter Boyer, who wrote an enlightening analysis of the unfortunate ATF raid and the disastrous FBI assault, FBI officials played on the ignorance of the newly appointed Attorney General Janet Reno, who simply did not know enough about the situation, by failing to inform her of vital plans and information. By claiming that Koresh was carrying out acts of child abuse inside the compound, the FBI virtually forced Reno into ordering a paramilitary attack on the compound. Whether child abuse did or did not take place, we don't know. But we do know that the results of the assault were disastrous.

WE ARE LIVING IN A SIMULATION

According to simulation hypotheses or simulation theories, all of reality, including the Earth and the universe, is an artificial simulation, and most likely a computer-generated one. Some versions of the theory centre around the idea of a "simulated reality", a technology that would create a simulation realistic enough to convince its inhabitants that it was real.

There are various elaborations of this line of thought. One of the leading thinkers on the subject is philosopher Nick Bostrom, who published a paper about it in 2003 entitled "Are You Living in a Computer Simulation?" He takes as a starting point the fact that many science-fiction authors and technologists have predicted that, in the future, huge amounts of computing power will be available. Supposing that these predictions prove to be correct, he posits that later generations might use these super-powerful computers to run detailed simulations of their ancestors. If the people in these simulations were conscious, then it would make it possible that "the vast majority of minds like ours do not belong to the original race but rather to people simulated by the advanced descendants of an original race". Bostrom concludes his argument by stating that, if this were the case, it would be rational for us to think that we are the simulated minds (rather than the original biological ones), and therefore, if we don't believe we are living in a simulation, we are not entitled to believe that we will have descendants who will run lots of such simulations of their ancestors.

The simulation theory has a firm presence in popular culture, having appeared as a central plot device in many science-fiction stories and films, such as *World on a Wire*, *Total Recall* and perhaps most famously the 1999 movie *The Matrix*. It also has some famous supporters, such as SpaceX boss Elon Musk, who said in an interview: "If you assume any rate of improvement at all, games will eventually be indistinguishable from reality... We're most likely in a simulation." And scientists are now reportedly looking for ways to test the theory, devising experiments that could distinguish physical reality from a simulation.

There are some less philosophically and scientifically based explorations of the simulation theory that appear regularly on internet forums. Here is a selection:

- Ghost hauntings and alien sightings are in fact glitches in the simulation.

- The reason that we've never encountered aliens is that they have figured out a way to escape from the simulation we are in.

- When electrons are fired at a photosensitive screen through slits in a copper plate (an exercise known as the double-slit experiment), it usually produces an interference pattern that indicates the electrons behave in a wavelike manner. Yet when the experiment is conducted under observation, the electrons behave like particles rather than waves, and there's no interference pattern. This apparently shows that in our simulation, resources are conserved by only rendering certain things when the simulation knows we're looking at them.

- The fact that we are facing an imminent climate crisis could be because we are in fact a simulated civilization created to help our creators figure out how to solve their own climate crisis.

- Some people say they recall TV coverage of Nelson Mandela's death in the 1980s, when in fact he died in 2013. Dubbed the "Mandela Effect", this is taken as evidence that whoever is in charge of our simulation is altering the past.

- Donald Trump's election, Brexit and the 2017 Oscars envelope mix-up are cited to prove that we are in a malfunctioning simulation – or that whoever is control of the simulation is clearly messing with us.

WILLIAM SHAKESPEARE

Romeo and Juliet, *Henry V*, *A Midsummer Night's Dream*, *As You Like It* and *The Tempest*: these are just some of the much-celebrated works penned by William Shakespeare, the iconic English wordsmith. Or was someone else behind the plays? Is Shakespeare history's greatest literary hoax?

There are those who believe that it was not actually Shakespeare who wrote the portfolio of classics that is credited to Stratford-upon-Avon's most famous son. Is the lack of written evidence for Shakespeare's existence, aside from his plays, proof that he was a work of fiction? How can the modestly educated Shakespeare's extensive knowledge of languages and travel be explained? So who was responsible?

Christopher Marlowe is one candidate put forward as the real hand behind the likes of *Othello* and *The Merchant of Venice*. Marlowe was also a sixteenth-century poet and is a celebrated Elizabethan tragedian in his own right. His death in 1593, after being fatally stabbed in a brawl in Deptford, would preclude him from being the author of the works of Shakespeare, but some consider that he faked his own demise in order to avoid arrest for blasphemy and to hide from debt collectors with murderous intent. From the sanctuary of anonymity, he is said to have penned the plays and sonnets accredited to his peer, who some believe was merely a village actor that Marlowe employed as part of his cover. A copyist named Thomas Walsingham is also thought to be complicit in the deception. In order to stop his identity being discovered through his handwriting, Marlowe employed Walsingham to copy out his manuscripts. Such a scam would explain why Shakespeare's first drafts were near perfect.

Sir Francis Bacon is another figure widely considered to have been the "real" Shakespeare. Allusions to his duplicity in his letters, where he describes himself as a "concealed poet", have been singled out by theorists as evidence of his trickery. Others allege that he took the pen name to ensure anonymity, as his aristocratic heritage would never have allowed him true literary fame. The only Shakespeare notebook ever found is said to be Bacon's *Promus*. Bacon's name is even said to appear in Shakespeare's works.

Edward de Vere, 17th Earl of Oxford, is suggested by some to be responsible for the Shakespearean catalogue. Again, it is de Vere's aristocratic heritage that demanded the pseudonym, as it was considered shameful for a man of such stature to write for public theatre at the time. His classical education, and similarities between the plays and his life, are supposed proof of his authorship.

Or was it Henry Neville, a distant relative of Shakespeare, whose nickname was Falstaff – a character that appears in three plays?

It has even been alleged that Shakespeare was not a man at all, but that the world's most famous playwright was no less than Queen Elizabeth I, a highly intelligent woman whose greatest legacy may actually have been the duping of centuries of historians, and the production of the greatest catalogue of English literature.

WOLFGANG AMADEUS MOZART

"Mozart is dead... Because his body swelled up after death, some people believe that he was poisoned... Now that he is dead the Viennese will at last realize what they had lost in him..."

So ran a report from a Prague correspondent in a Berlin newspaper less than a month after Wolfgang Amadeus Mozart's death. Conspiracy theories were mooted immediately. Questions of who had killed possibly the greatest composer ever to have lived have intrigued historians attempting to unravel the threads of the mystery surrounding such a premature death.

One theory suggests that Antonio Salieri, the long-time arch-rival of Mozart, killed him. Indeed, toward the end of his own life, Salieri seems to have lost his reason and attempted suicide. From that moment until his own death, rumour had it that he had in fact confessed to the murder of Mozart. However, what could Salieri have gained from Mozart's death?

WOLFGANG AMADEUS MOZART

Although Mozart was by far the superior composer of the two, in material terms Salieri actually had the better-paid job as imperial kapellmeister, a post which, no doubt, Mozart would have dearly loved. Not only did he have a better salary, but also more opportunities for creativity in terms of having the freedom to compose. At the time, Saleri's operas had at least as fine a reputation as Mozart's. Materially, it would seem that Mozart would have had a stronger urge to kill Salieri. As the film *Amadeus* would have it, Salieri's wrath against his rival could have been inspired purely out of jealousy; while Salieri toiled away laboriously to produce his art, which was, in the end, no more than second-rate, Mozart worked apparently effortlessly, achieving what was quite indisputably the work of a genius.

Others would point the finger at the Freemasons, with whom Mozart had become involved in his youth. *Die Zauberflöte* is essentially a Masonic opera, and shows the artist's struggle against Christianity, and in particular the Catholic Church. But at the same time, the Masonic content of the opera is constantly put to question. Mozart did not take Masonic word as law. He came from an unquestionably Christian tradition and, moreover, a Christian chorale may be heard in the duet of the armed men in the opera. Sarastro, the archetypal Masonic figure, is not good through and through, but appears as a kidnapper. Apparently Mozart had planned to establish a new order, a rival to the Freemasons, going by the name of "Die Grotte", suggesting that his relationship with the Masons was not entirely happy. He had allegedly taken his clarinettist friend, and sometime Mason, Anton Stadler into his confidence and had consequently been betrayed by him. As a final possible point of evidence, it would seem strange that the Masons made no financial contribution toward his funeral expenses and were prepared to let Mozart be buried in a pauper's grave.

YITZHAK RABIN

When Israeli Prime Minister Yitzhak Rabin was assassinated in 1995 after a peace rally in Tel Aviv, media coverage of the event was pretty clear cut: a Jewish Israeli student named Yigal Amir was swiftly apprehended by onlookers and confessed to the killing. Amir was said to have been opposed to Rabin's signing of the Oslo Accords and believed he was acting in the best interests of the country by removing Rabin. But conspiracy theorists have refused to accept this explanation at face value.

Two years after the death of Rabin, *HaTzofeh*, an Israeli right-wing newspaper, published a story highlighting a conspiracy theory being put forward on the internet by a man named Uzi Barkan. At the same time, the government released previously unpublished findings of a commission that investigated the assassination. Government officials who have read the report say that the document reveals that an agent of the government security service, Shin Bet, urged the killer to shoot Rabin.

Once the document had been released, Benjamin Netanyahu's government demanded further investigations into the parts of the report that were still unavailable. It seemed that the most suspicious individual was a man called Avishai Raviv and he was immediately prosecuted. Raviv was seen as a militant right-wing radical who was known for taking teenagers away on "summer camps" and then indoctrinating them with his political ideas. It was alleged that Raviv had befriended Amir in this way several years before, and then persuaded him to act as an assassin. Whether Raviv was or wasn't behind the murder of Rabin, the fact that he knew Amir at all is notable, and the fact that he may have acted as some kind of mentor to him in the past places him under even greater suspicion.

Investigations into the murder were hampered by those government officials who claimed that the inconsistencies surrounding the murder were nothing unusual and that it is almost impossible to find a crime where the facts are all clearly defined and laid out. Chemi Shalev, an Israeli political analyst, said that the suggestion that Shin Bet planned the murder is "outlandish… But the question of Raviv as an agent who somehow incited Amir, or whether the Shin Bet went too far in provoking incidents against the prime minister, that part of it is a question being asked by many people, even people on the left."